# WEAPON

# MG 34 AND MG 42 MACHINE GUNS

CHRIS McNAB

Series Editor Martin Pegler

T0322584

OSPREY PUBLISHING
Bloomsbury Publishing Plc

Kemp House, Chawley Park, Cumnor Hill, Oxford OX2 9PH, UK
29 Earlsfort Terrace, Dublin 2, Ireland
1385 Broadway, 5th Floor, New York, NY 10018, USA
Email: info@ospreypublishing.com
www.ospreypublishing.com

OSPREY is a trademark of Osprey Publishing Ltd

First published in Great Britain in 2012

A catalogue record for this book is available from the
British Library.

Print ISBN: 978 1 78096 008 1
ePDF: 978 1 78096 010 4
ePub: 978 1 78200 309 0

Page layout by Mark Holt
Index by Fionbar Lyons
Battlescene artwork by Ramiro Bujeiro
Cutaway by Alan Gilliland
Typeset in Sabon and Univers
Originated by PDQ Media, Bungay, UK
Printed and bound in India by Replika Press Private Ltd.

22 23 24 25 26    15 14 13 12 11 10 9 8

The Woodland Trust
Osprey Publishing supports the Woodland Trust, the UK's leading
woodland conservation charity.

www.ospreypublishing.com
To find out more about our authors and books visit our website.
Here you will find extracts, author interviews, details of
forthcoming events and the option to sign-up for our newsletter.

## Acknowledgements

I would like to thank Nick Reynolds and Tom Milner at Osprey,
and series editor Martin Pegler, for their expertise and support in
shaping this book for publication, and also to Ted Nevill of Cody
Images for providing many of the photographs. Thanks also go
to Bob Hurley in the United States for his advice early on in this
project about sources of information.

## Artist's note

Readers may care to note that the original paintings from which
the colour plates in this book were prepared are available for
private sale. All reproduction copyright whatsoever is retained
by the Publishers. All enquiries should be addressed to:

Ramiro Bujeiro,
C.C. 28,
1602 Florida,
Argentina

The Publishers regret that they can enter into no correspondence
upon this matter.

## Editor's note

For ease of comparison please refer to the following
conversion table:

1 mile = 1.6km
1yd = 0.9m
1ft = 0.3m
1in. = 2.54cm/25.4mm
1lb = 0.45kg

## Cover images

Courtesy Cody Images and Nikolaus von Nathusius.

# CONTENTS

# INTRODUCTION

Although in war all enemy weapons are potential sources of fear, some seem to have a deeper grip on the imagination than others. The AK-47, for example, is actually no more lethal than most other small arms in its class, but popular notoriety and Hollywood representations tend to credit it with superior power and lethality. Similarly, the bayonet actually killed relatively few men in World War I, but the sheer thought of an enraged foe bearing down on you with more than 30cm of sharpened steel was the stuff of nightmares to both sides. In some cases, however, fear has been perfectly justified. During both world wars, for example, artillery caused between 59 and 80 per cent of all casualties (depending on your source), and hence took a justifiable top slot in surveys of most feared tools of violence.

The subjects of this book – the MG 34 and MG 42, plus derivatives – are interesting case studies within the scale of soldiers' fears. Regarding the latter weapon, a US wartime information movie once declared that the gun's 'bark was worse than its bite', no doubt a well-intentioned comment intended to reduce mounting concern among US troops about the firepower of this astonishing gun. In fact, the exact opposite was probably true. Firing at a cyclical rate of 1,200rpm, the MG 42 had a truly appalling bite. An on-target burst of just half a second could slash through a man with no fewer than ten 7.92×57mm high-velocity rounds, each delivering dreadful injuries, and at ranges of well over a kilometre. The MG 34 fired with less pace – up to 900rpm – but was also a proficient killing engine in trained hands.

Eyewitness accounts of both the MG 34 and, more particularly, the MG 42 tend to speak of the weapons with an almost hushed respect. To take a case in point, here is a memory from former Polish freedom fighter Marian S. Mazgai, who himself became an enthusiastic operator of captured MG 42s:

A unit from the Jedrus company pushed toward the end of the road that went in the direction of Momocicha, but when it reached the top of the elevation that divided it from the enemy, the German machine-gun fire, from a nearby windmill, forced it to hit the ground. I will never forget that heavy German machine-gun fire that almost cost me my life. When the Germans fired at our unit from the windmill as well as from its vicinity, we responded with our fire. I happened to fire a German-made machine gun MG 42 from a fine position. At the same time, I was doing everything possible to discover the German position from which the enemy was firing at us with the same kind of machine guns, MG 42s. According to my humble estimation, model MG 42 was the best machine gun used in World War II. (Mazgai 2008: 211)

The MG 42 represented the ultimate in German infantry firepower. It became the scourge of the Allies, and was justly feared by all those who faced it. (Cody Images)

A two-man German machine-gun team man their MG 34 in Kharkov on the Eastern Front. Note the three ammunition cans stacked nearby, each containing up to 300 rounds. (Cody Images)

Mazgai makes quite clear the extent to which the MG 42 fire was burned into his memory. As we shall see later in this book, other soldiers share similar dark memories, particularly relating to the grim intensity of the MG 42 bullet stream, and its ability to suppress movement and kill in volume. Mazgai also makes a bold statement here, arguing that the MG 42 was the 'best machine gun used in World War II'. Soldiers can be hyperbolic, especially when describing a weapon for which they have affection, but in the case of the MG 42 the statement can be backed by argument. The older MG 34 was a decent enough machine gun in itself, part of a radical new concept in firearms design. The MG 42, however, was a masterpiece at both engineering and tactical levels. Applied intelligently by a motivated machine-gun team, a single MG 42 was quite capable of driving an entire American company to ground and holding them there, or of carving up a Soviet infantry assault on the Eastern Front. Hence in the case of the MG 42, any fear was quite justified.

The story of the MG 34 and MG 42 concerns a seminal step forward in machine-gun design. By the time the MG 34 emerged into the German Army in the 1930s, the machine gun as a specific type was just under 40 years old, having been born in the late 1880s in the form of the Maxim Gun. During the early 20th century and World War I, new operating mechanisms and the creation of the light machine gun (LMG) introduced some diversification into the machine-gun format. Yet depending on their physical size and their firepower, individual machine guns were still limited in terms of their tactical options. What the MG 34 represented was the physical embodiment of the German quest for the *Einheitsmaschinengewehr* (universal machine gun), a weapon that was capable of fulfilling a multitude of combat roles simply by modifying its mount and its sights. The MG 42 then took the *Einheitsmaschinengewehr* principle to even greater heights. With its high rate of fire, battlefield functionality, rugged design, battlefield effect and ease of use, it could adapt to roles that ranged from supporting an infantry assault weapon to delivering short-range anti-aircraft (AA) fire. Few equivalents on the part of the Allies were ever as convincing in terms of flexibility. Hence the MG 34 and the MG 42 laid the groundwork for many other wartime and post-war machine guns, notwithstanding the direct variants of the weapon that endure in service to this day.

The story of the MG 34 and MG 42 is undoubtedly technologically fascinating. The MG 34, like the MG 42, did not simply emerge from a design void, but evolved from a succession of experimental weapons and concepts. Each step of the journey required innovation in thought and industry to accomplish. Yet from the battlefield perspective, it is hard to escape the sheer dreadfulness of the *Einheitsmaschinengewehr*'s effect on the human form. For both of these machine guns were created with attrition and destruction as their end game, and in those objectives the MG 34 and MG 42 were singularly successful.

The MG 42 has been a truly enduring design in firearms history. Here a US Army soldier, based in Egypt in 1983, test-fires a 7.62mm MG 42/59 variant, licence-produced in Sudan. (Cody Images)

# DEVELOPMENT
## The 'universal' machine gun

World War I was truly the conflict that confirmed the place of the machine gun in modern warfare. Apart from artillery, the machine gun was the most effective means of both suppression and attrition of the enemy. For the Germans, like the British, the Maxim Gun formed the inspiration for their principal machine gun between 1914 and 1917, the MG 08. Working on the principle of short recoil, the water-cooled MG 08 was powerful (it fired the 7.92×57mm German rifle cartridge) and could rattle reliably through 250-round fabric belts at a rate of 300–450rpm. It was, however, a true *heavy* machine gun (HMG). The gun alone, with its water jacket full, weighed 26kg and its Schlitten 08 sled carriage added another 32kg. As such, the MG 08 was suited only to emplaced, sustained-fire roles, not for being nimbly transported around the battlefield.

### THE LIGHT MACHINE GUN CONCEPT

The Entente Powers also had their own heavyweight weapons – the British Vickers and the Russian M1910 placed similar burdens on their gun teams – but during the war they were quicker at embracing a new concept, that of the light machine gun (LMG). As its name suggested, the LMG's *raison d'être* was portability, which meant that the firepower of a machine gun could be taken forward conveniently by assaulting troops, and moved between positions for tactical fire support. The US-designed, British-adopted Lewis Gun was arguably the best of the LMG class in World War I. It weighed 11.8kg, was air-cooled (thereby removing the weight of a water jacket), worked on gas-operation (a particularly light system) and was fed from a 47-round pan magazine. The Lewis was far from perfect

– it suffered from stoppages and its fixed barrel meant that it could not deliver the sustained fire of an HMG. (Sustained fire, which involves frequent, repeated long bursts of automatic fire, causes barrels to heat up rapidly to the point when firing has to stop to let the barrel cool.) Yet it could be carried quickly across the battlefield, emplaced in seconds on its bipod mount, and then deliver burst fire at rates of 550rpm.

Other LMGs of the war included the French 8mm Chauchat Mle 1915 (admittedly a truly terrible weapon) and the American Browning Automatic Rifle (BAR). Alongside the Lewis Gun, such weapons proved the LMG concept in theory if not always in practice. In 1915, the Germans recognized that they also needed an LMG in frontline hands. Rather than work up a new design, however, they chose to adapt the MG 08. The Spandau Arsenal produced the MG 08/15, which was the MG 08 but fitted with a bipod, pistol grip and shoulder stock. The MG 08/15 was produced in large numbers (130,000 in total), and it certainly headed towards being a true LMG in layout and tactical applications. Yet it remained very heavy – 21kg with its water jacket full – which meant that it could never compare to the battlefield portability of a Lewis. (Lewis Guns were much-prized acquisitions by German machine-gun teams for this reason.) A futile attempt to remedy the problem was the late-war MG 08/18, which was air-cooled but managed to be only 1kg lighter than the MG 08/15. Clearly, the Maxim Gun was not a sound basis for an LMG.

There were other, less prominent, German machine guns in World War I that showed more promising understandings of tactical firepower. The air-cooled 7.92mm Bergmann MG 15nA weighed a more manageable 13kg, utilized a bipod mount and was fed from a 200-round metal-link belt (a big improvement over the fabric belts, which were prone to stretching and cartridge extraction problems when wet) contained in an assault drum. Despite its qualities, it was overshadowed by the production volumes of the MG 08/15, and largely relegated to use in limited numbers on the Italian Front. Similarly sidelined were Louis Schmeisser's Dreyse MG 10 and MG 15. Both were water-cooled, short-recoil weapons, but

The MG 08/15 (bottom) was the rather misguided attempt to create a light machine gun from the standard MG 08 (top). Weight savings over the MG 08 were minimal, and it was a cumbersome beast to use in the assault. (Cody Images)

The machine-gunner's burden. During one of the Aisne battles of World War I, a German unit lugs two MG 08 guns up an embankment during an assault. Each gun weighed 26kg, hence they were suited for little more than static defence roles. (Cody Images)

the MG 15 had a bipod and even a monopod, as opposed to the MG 10's tripod. By using an accelerator and recoil buffer, the Dreyse guns also delivered a fast rate of fire, higher than the average. More significantly, just before the end of the war, an air-cooled version of this weapon was produced, known as the Dreyse *Muskete* or the MG 15.

Despite such developments, the fact remained that Germany ended World War I with little more than modified HMGs as its primary infantry support weapons. But conceptual seeds were sown during the conflict. In 1916, the German Army's ordnance experts began to discuss the idea of the *Einheitsmaschinengewehr*. They envisaged a weapon that was capable of fulfilling a number of roles, effectively combining the tactical remit of both the MG 08 and MG 08/15, and also occupying the ground of what would be termed a medium machine gun (MMG). (Definitions vary, but an MMG is typically viewed as a belt-fed machine gun, firing a full-power rifle cartridge, but capable of switching between bipod and tripod mounts.) The exigencies of war quickly stopped this plan from finding practical realization. It would be revisited in earnest during the 1920s and '30s, however, as Europe once again began to prepare for war.

## FORERUNNERS

In the immediate aftermath of World War I, the German Army's capability to produce and stockpile machine guns seemed irrevocably stunted by the Versailles Treaty. The Reichswehr ('Imperial Defence'; the German armed forces from 1919 to 1931) was limited to possessing 792 MMGs and 1,134 HMGs. These restrictions were subsequently raised slightly, and the Reichswehr could also draw on tens of thousands of MG 08s and variants, secreted away among various arsenals around the country. Furthermore, history now knows that Germany was largely able to circumvent prohibitions on all manner of weapons development, by utilizing German-owned or partially controlled foreign-based companies. Hence while only one German company was allowed to manufacture machine guns – Simson & Cie near Erfurt – further design, development and production work continued in Spain, the Netherlands, the Soviet Union, Sweden and Switzerland. The most important organizations in terms of machine guns were Waffenfabrik Solothurn AG in Switzerland, over which Rheinmetall gained control in 1929, and Steyr in Austria, with which Rheinmetall also established a close working partnership (and possibly commercial control). Through such means, Germany embarked on a new phase of machine-gun development during the 1930s.

While there were continuing efforts to refine the MG 08/15, the *Einheitsmaschinengewehr* concept was practically, if not yet consciously, revived in other weapons. The Dreyse guns were tinkered with, producing the Gerät 13a and Gerät 14. The latter was a large, water-cooled, closed-bolt MMG, mounted on a tripod, but the former weapon was much more closely aligned to the *Einheitsmaschinengewehr* aspiration. It was air-cooled, with a slender ventilated barrel jacket and bipod mount. Most conspicuously, it was fed from a top-mounted 25-round flat pan magazine.

The Dreyse guns formed the foundation of a gun that took a definitive step in the direction of the MG 34, which was still some years away. From them emerged the MG 13, Germany's first officially produced post-World War I machine gun. It was very similar to the Dreyse *Muskete* and Gerät 13a, but took a 25-round curved box magazine – later a 75-round *Patronentrommel* (double-drum) magazine – and could be mounted on either a bipod or, for AA use, a tripod. A shorter version was built for applications to armoured vehicles, and was known as the MG 13k (the 'k' refers to *kurz*, meaning 'short'). An interesting feature was fire selection via a rocking trigger: single shots were fired by pulling the top section of the trigger, while full-auto fire came from drawing on the bottom section.

RAF pilots entertain themselves with a captured German MG 15. The MG 15 was one of several weapons the design of which fed into that of the MG 34. Features shared with the MG 34 included the 75-round snail drum feed and rotating-receiver barrel change. (Cody Images)

Tactical flexibility through mount arrangements is apparent in the MG 13, but there were many more steps to take before the *Einheitsmaschinengewehr* concept was finally realized in the MG 34. While visible production of machine guns continued through Simson & Cie (the guns were actually manufactured at the Rheinmetall plant in Sömmerda), other weapons were emerging. Exhaustive coverage of these developments is not possible here, but a summary of key stages shows something of the journey towards the MG 34. Via Solothurn (although originally designed by Louis Stange at Rheinmetall) came the short-recoil S 2-200 (or the MG 30S), which took on the MG 13's rocking trigger mechanism (the S 2-200 had a full-auto rate of 800rpm) but simplified the barrel-change process somewhat. It also led to an aircraft-mounted variant, the MG 15, which was also later used among ground troops in the last years of World War II, when the German Army's supply of machine guns began to run dry. The German firearms designer Heinrich Vollmer also submitted various prototypes to the *Waffen und Gerät* (Weapons and Equipment) authorities during the 1920s and early 1930s. Via the Mauser concern, these included the Mauser-Vollmer MV31, a reliable short-recoil LMG that could feed from either drums or magazines. Mauser also produced the LMG32, which alongside the S 2-200 was one of the stepping-stones to the MG 34. Designed by Ernst Altenburger, little is actually known about the details of this weapon, just that it was recoil-operated with a quick-change barrel, plus it had a two-piece bolt that locked onto a barrel extension, both features that would be found in the MG 34.

## THE MG 34 EMERGES

The actual steps by which the MG 34 came to be designed and adopted for German Army service are not entirely clear, due to the destruction of related documents during World War II. However, one of the best guides to the overall steps behind its creation is Louis Stange, who wrote the following account in 1941:

> In 1932 the *Reichsministerium* [Reich Ministry] ordered several companies, including Rheinmetall, to develop a new *Einheitsmaschinengewehr*. This new weapon had to be able to fulfill the duties hitherto allocated to the specific classes of weapons known as the Heavy Machinegun, the Light Machinegun, the Armoured Pillbox Machinegun, and Anti-Aircraft Machinegun. The following specifications were set: light weight; simplified operation; quick-change barrel; single-shot capability as well as two [fast and slow] cyclic rates. The development of this weapon set the standard for co-operation in the German armament industry, and the task at hand was completed through the professional guidance of the *Waffenamt* [Weapons Procurement Office]. The result, the MG34, wherein Rheinmetall's Sömmerda plant had a significant influence, reflected the *Reichsministerium* specifications in all respects. (Quoted in Myrvang 2002: 30)

This potted history shows clearly how tactical imperatives led the way in the development of the MG 34. It also evokes the sheer range of challenges that must have faced the Mauser-Werke designers in meeting the *Reichsministerium* specifications, not only in terms of the gun itself but also regarding the mounts that had to adapt that gun to different roles. Here was a firearm that had to be practical in scenarios ranging from a light infantry assault through to indirect fire at major enemy troop concentrations. That the designers managed to fulfil this brief is testimony to the extraordinary innovation demonstrated repeatedly by German weapon designers during the 1930s.

Stange's account, however, is very cursory regarding the long gestation of the MG 34 from specifications to final design and adoption. The gun went through three main variations before it was adopted. The first variation, of which only 300 were made in or around 1935, had distinct differences from the final production model. In terms of external appearance, it had a steeper top cover hump and an aluminium knob for a cocking handle. The pistol-grip assembly was also quite different in fittings, and featured an adjustable rate-of-fire device that allowed the gun to switch between 600rpm and 1,000rpm (at least according to the scale, whereas the reality was 400rpm and 900rpm). The earliest MG 34s also had reversible feed trays, by which the gun could be adjusted for either left- or right-handed feed. The second variation (2,000 guns) changed the pistol-grip fittings to use split pins and bushings, as in the final production variant, and the rate-of-fire adjuster was moved from the left-hand grip panel to the root of the trigger guard.

The MG 34 was now approaching its final variation, described in more detail below. It was finally adopted for service in the German Army on 24 January 1939, and it was intended to replace all MG 08s, MG 08/15s, MG 13s and any other machine guns in German Army service. This process took some time, and it was not until late 1941 that the MG 34 was distributed throughout the German field army, by which time the gun had been thoroughly tested in war.

The MG 34 machine gun. Distinguishing visual features of the MG 34 were the flared flash hider at the muzzle, the slender ventilated barrel jacket, the pillar-type iron sight and the flared stock. (Cody Images)

## THE MG 34 DESCRIBED

The MG 34 is a complicated gun at every level – a fact that would lead eventually to its being superseded by the MG 42 – but there was no denying the inventiveness and engineering that went into its creation. In basic overview, the MG 34 is a short-recoil, air-cooled machine gun, firing the redoubtable 7.92×57mm Mauser cartridge. In terms of feed, the MG 34 had two options: the two-section 75-round Doppeltrommel 15 saddle magazine – actually known as the Patronentrommel 34 in the context of the MG 34 – or 250-round metal-link belt. From November 1939, a 50-round belt could also be contained in a *Gurttrommel* (belt drum). (Switching between the saddle drum and belt feed required changing the feedway top cover.) The Patronentrommel 34 was a complicated piece of engineering, designed so that the cartridges were fed in from alternate sides, to prevent the weight distribution shifting to one side during firing. It was also fiddly to load and unload, hence its use waned as the war went on.

The MG 34 is a quick-firing gun, up to 900rpm. (The gun tended to fire faster from the saddle-drum magazine than a standard belt, due to the spring loading of the former.) The distinction between single-shot and full-auto fire is made not via a selector switch, as on most machine guns, but via trigger pull: semi-auto fire is delivered via the upper part of the trigger, and full-auto via the lower part. The physical arrangements for this system are mechanically complex to say the least, and such complexity was mirrored in the operating system itself. As noted, the MG 34 is a short-recoil weapon, meaning that the action is cycled by the forces of recoil, but that the recoil travel of the barrel and action before unlocking is less than the length of the entire cartridge. When the MG 34's trigger is pulled (assuming that the gun has been cocked and ammunition is in the feed tray), the bolt assembly is driven forward under the power of the recoil spring. The bolt assembly itself consists of two parts: the bolt and a rotating bolt head. As the bolt assembly goes forward, it strips a round from the belt and drives it into the chamber. As it does so, the bolt head rotates via the interaction of rollers on cams in a locking collar attached to the rear of the barrel. By the end of the travel forward, the rollers on the bolt head lock into interrupted threads in the locking collar, and the extractor pops up to grip the rim of the cartridge. The action of bolt locking also releases the firing pin, which is driven forward to strike the cartridge primer and fire the gun.

As the bullet leaves the MG 34's barrel, gas pressure acts on the booster cone at the front of the gun, driving the barrel and locked bolt assembly back by about 2cm, as the bolt head begins to rotate in the reverse direction and is unlocked in just 1.5cm of travel. It is also at this stage in the action that the firing-pin mechanism is cocked for the next shot. Once the barrel and bolt are unlocked, the bolt assembly travels to the rear of the gun, while the barrel returns to the front via a barrel return spring mechanism. The spent cartridge case is drawn from the chamber by the extractor, and ejected through an aperture just in front of the trigger guard, on the underside of the receiver. The recoil spring eventually arrests the rearward movement of the bolt, and if the full-auto mode is engaged the

gun will then repeat the cycle until the trigger is released or it runs out of ammunition. As all this is taking place, the motion of the bolt also powers the feed mechanism, which drives the belt through the gun.

This short description does not do full justice to the sheer complexity of the mechanical arrangements playing out while the MG 34 was firing, running through its entire cycle at a rate of 15 times every second.

Naturally, a quick-change barrel was an important feature of such a fast-firing weapon as the MG 34, with a change being recommended after every 250 rounds of rapid or sustained fire. The process of performing this action was straightforward enough, particularly when compared to many previous machine guns. First, the gun has to be cocked with the bolt held to the rear and the safety lever set on 'Safe'. Then the operator depresses the receiver latch beneath the rear sight, which allows the entire receiver to pivot on an axial pin through nearly 180 degrees, at which point the barrel slides out when the stock is angled down towards the ground. (When the MG 34 was on fixed mounts, such as heavy tripods, the gun could not be tipped, so the barrel had to be hooked out with any convenient object.) A new barrel is then inserted into place, and the receiver swung back into position. The entire process would take about 10–15 seconds in the hands of a trained crew.

The quick-change barrel of the MG 34 was integral to the fulfilment of the *Einheitsmaschinengewehr* brief, as it meant that the frequency of barrel changes could be adapted to the fire mission, from occasional suppressive bursts to indirect sustained fire at area targets. But the other factor in this equation was mounts, as a May 1943 US Army intelligence document noted:

A German infantry unit crouch behind a PzKpfw I during the invasion of Poland in 1939. Four of the visible men are armed with MG 34s, ready loaded with 50-round belts. The soldier immediately behind the rear of the tank carries a spare barrel in a container. (Cody Images)

The *M.G. 34*, machine gun, model 34, is not directly comparable to any U.S. weapon. It can be fired without a mount, or it can be mounted on a bipod for use as a light machine gun, on a tripod for use as a heavy machine gun, and on a special antiaircraft mount or on the standard tripod mount with adapter and special sight for use as an antiaircraft gun, as well as on numerous other types of mounts on tanks and other vehicles. Consequently, this all-purpose gun is the most common German automatic weapon in use by the German armed forces. Every infantry squad, and many other types of small German units, can be expected to be armed with the *M.G. 34*. (US Army 1943: III. 12)

This quotation reveals an implicit respect, even nervousness, towards the MG 34, the writer recognizing that the US military has nothing of similar flexibility. Simply changing between one of a number of mounts altered the very tactical essence of the MG 34. For standard infantry use, there were two primary mounts. The MG 34's own integral bipod, mounted near the muzzle or (less commonly) near the receiver, was of superior design, not least because it was articulated to allow the gunner to traverse the weapon without lifting the bipod feet from the ground. The principal tripod was the similarly excellent Lafette 34, which featured a 'softmount' reciprocating spring cradle that absorbed the MG 34's recoil, meaning that the gun stayed accurate even under sustained fire. Combined with a fully adjustable height system (including an AA fire extension), a searching-fire device (automatically adjusting the elevation of the gun up and down during firing to deepen the 'beaten zone') plus precision adjustability, the softmount system of the Lafette 34 meant that infantry could saturate a target with complete controllability.

There were numerous other specialist mounts for the MG 34. The Dreibein 34, for example, was a simple high-standing tripod for mounting the gun in anti-aircraft mode. There were also mounts for bicycles, motorcycle sidecars, tanks and armoured vehicles (ball and pintle mounts),

An MG 34 captured and put into use by a British commando at Ranville, Normandy, in 1944. The screw in the centre of the bipod legs allowed the adjustment of the width of the legs on the ground. (Cody Images)

**MG 34 specifications**

| | |
|---|---|
| Calibre | 7.92×57mm Mauser |
| Length | 1,219mm |
| Weight (empty) | 12.1kg |
| Barrel | 627mm, 4 grooves, rh |
| Feed | 50/250-round belts; 50-round drum; 75-round saddle drum |
| Action | short recoil |
| Rate of fire | 800–900rpm |
| Muzzle velocity | 755m/sec |

fortress positions, boat decks and even assault gliders. MG 34s were mounted in multiple-gun arrangements, particularly on vehicles, for AA defence. One of the most distinctive configurations was the MG Wagen 36, basically a horse-drawn two-wheeled cart fitted with two MG 34s on the Zwillingsockel 36 twin mount. It was obvious that Germany had truly found its first *Einheitsmaschinengewehr*. (Mounts and their use are discussed in more detail below.)

## RATIONALIZATION AND THE MG 42

As indicated above, the MG 34 was a resounding success in terms of equipping the German Army with an *Einheitsmaschinengewehr*. Total production of the MG 34 from the late 1930s until the end of the war was in the region of 450,000 units, although precise figures are not possible to obtain. Furthermore, although the MG 42 would from 1942 take over as the new generation of infantry machine gun, the MG 42 was not suited to mounting in many specialized fortification and armoured vehicle mounts, hence the MG 34 retained a rationale for its continued existence. There was also a faster-firing variant, the MG 34/41 – known as the MG 34S – developed to provide more potent suppressive capabilities. By shortening and lightening the barrel, increasing the strength of the recoil spring and installing a more potent recoil booster, the MG 34/41's designers created a gun with a 1,200rpm rate of fire, which placed extreme demands on the MG 34's mechanism. Few were actually manufactured (about 300), and all went to the Eastern Front in 1942.

As we shall see in the next chapter, the MG 34 proved itself in battle. Yet it was not a perfect weapon, certainly not in the context of practical wartime realities. The complex mechanisms and the production method, which relied principally on expensive machining processes, were not ideal for rapid production under pressure, nor for the best utilization of stretched supplies of raw materials. Furthermore, the MG 34 was not at its best in very dirty environments, of which North Africa and the Eastern Front offered plenty of examples, and was therefore prone to jamming unless kept scrupulously clean. Concerns about cost and reliability had actually surfaced well before the war, in 1935, and three companies were

A soldier on the Eastern Front carries his MG 42 over his shoulder. Weighing 11.5kg, the MG 42 was remarkably light for the firepower that it could deliver in combat. (Cody Images)

commissioned to develop a new *Einheitsmaschinengewehr*, with a simpler design and a greater use of cost-effective metal-stamping techniques.

Of the three companies involved in the process – Metall & Lackierwarenfabrik Johannes Großfuß AG, Rheinmetall-Borsig and Stübgen – it was Großfuß who came through with the most promising design, despite having little experience in weapons design compared to the other two contenders. Prototypes were submitted between 1938 and 1941, and they quickly ran ahead of the competition. Constructed virtually entirely of stamped sheet metal, the new gun could be produced with 75 man-hours of labour, as opposed to 150 hours for the MG 34, and reduced costs per gun by nearly 25 per cent. They incorporated a lightning-fast barrel-change mechanism and an innovative roller-locked mechanism, and with a blistering rate of fire of up to 1,500rpm the MG 39 and MG 39/41 guns were utterly convincing, so much so that Adolf Hitler himself ordered the gun's rapid production in December 1941. Field trials of 1,500 guns proved the weapon in action, and it entered full production in 1942 as the now-infamous MG 42.

The fast-pulsing heart of the MG 42 was its new roller-locked bolt mechanism. Gone was the rotating-bolt configuration of the MG 34; the MG 42's mechanism worked entirely on a flat plane. The MG 42's bolt assembly consists of two main parts: the bolt housing and the bolt head, the latter featuring two locking rollers that correspond with locking grooves on the end of a barrel extension, and a firing pin running through the centre. The MG 42 is an open-bolt weapon (open-bolt firing allows for improved airflow and cooling on a fast-firing weapon), and when a belt is loaded and the gun is cocked, pulling the trigger releases the bolt assembly under the power of the recoil spring. As the bolt travels forwards, it catches a round from the cartridge belt and pushes it forwards into the chamber. The bolt head's locking rollers are kept pressed inwards by glide rails in the receiver until the bolt head enters the barrel extension, at which point the rollers are pushed outwards into the barrel extension recesses to lock the gun for firing. Once the rollers lock outwards, the firing pin is free to move forwards and ignite the cartridge.

As with the recoil phase of the MG 34, the MG 42's barrel and bolt now recoil together a short distance. The two components then unlock as curved cams push the bolt-head rollers inwards. The bolt continues to the rear under the mounting pressure of the recoil spring, while the barrel is driven forward via a recuperator spring. Ejection takes place during this phase; the bolt head extractor grips the rim of the cartridge case and pulls

'Light Machine Gun, Cal .30, T24'. The Saginaw Steering Gear Division of General Motors Corporation (GMC) was commissioned to undertake the study, 'with a view of developing a weapon of this type for our own use' (letter from the War Department, 12 June 1943). The guns went through many modifications other than calibre, including the fitting of a US M3 tripod and of BAR sights, and the use of a much heavier bolt to handle the powerful cartridge. Test results were not promising, as this report of 12 February 1944 revealed:

> Unsatisfactory gun functioning led to substitution and changes of various component parts in an effort to place the weapon in a condition to continue the test, but all attempts failed ... Firing was suspended by verbal authorization of Major C Balleisen, OCO, when it became evident that the weapon required further development before being submitted to the rigorous standard Light Machine Gun test.
> ... In all, 1,583 rounds were fired, with a total of 51 malfunctions being recorded. The average cyclic rate of the weapon was 614 rpm ...
> (Aberdeen Proving Ground 1944; quoted in Myrvang 2002: 183)

The T24 was mooted as a possible replacement for the BAR, but the experiment ultimately came to nothing – conversion to the US .30cal round upset the integrity of the entire MG 42 design, so the project was abandoned. The MG 42 did, however, go on to influence the design of the belt-feed mechanism of the later M60 machine gun, introduced into US Army service in 1957.

It was in the post-war world that the MG 42 really went on to have a global influence. Many nations which had fought both alongside and against the Germans had been singularly impressed by the MG 42's combat qualities. Hence as states looked to re-equip themselves in the new world order, the MG 42/59 and MG3 were strong contenders in military trials.

The Italians, former wartime allies of Germany, licence-produced the MG 42/59 in 7.62mm calibre as the *Fucile Mitragliatore* through the Beretta company from 1963. Like the German weapons, the *Fucile Mitragliatore* found itself not only in the hands of infantry machine-gun teams, but also mounted on armoured vehicles, helicopters and even naval vessels. Although at the time of writing the Italian Army is shifting its loyalties to the Belgian FN Minimi as its standard infantry machine gun, Stabilimento Militare Armi Leggere Terni (SMALT) has produced a kit to adapt the MG 42/59 machine gun to 5.56×45mm NATO ammunition.

The list of countries that have used, manufactured or bought MG 42 derivatives goes well beyond Italy. In Yugoslavia, the MG 42 continued to thrive in the form of the M53, in effect a locally produced copy that went on to assist in Yugoslavia's bitter break-up in the 1990s. During the 1960s alone, Norway, Denmark, Indonesia, Pakistan, Sudan, Burma and Chile all adopted the 7.62mm MG 42/59. Turkey and Greece became licensed manufacturers. The Austrians took the MG 42/59 as the MG74,

Post-war Italian infantry conduct an exercise, the soldier at the front carrying the Italian licence-produced version of the MG 42/59. Italian use of the gun also extended to helicopter and armoured vehicle mounts. (Cody Images)

albeit with some significant adaptations, such as a single-shot capability and a modern polymer stock. In fact, it is noteworthy that during recent coalition operations in Afghanistan, 17 different member states have relied upon the MG 42/59 or MG3 for infantry firepower. Such longevity and popularity means that the MG 42 takes its rightful place alongside guns such as the Browning M2 as one of the most successful firearm designs in history.

A Norwegian soldier holds his MG3 secure as he goes into action aboard a UH-60 helicopter. The stock contour has scarcely changed since World War II, and is ideal for a solid two-handed grip. (US DoD)

then pushed the feed cover catch forwards and opened the top cover, placing the first round of the belt against the cartridge stops and then carefully closing the top cover again. Note that if the belt was in a belt drum, the drum needed to be attached to the feed block before loading.

Loading the MG 34 with the 75-round drum magazine necessitated a different approach. First, the feed cover and feed block were removed and replaced with a dedicated magazine holder. The magazine was then placed onto the magazine holder, front end down, and pressed into place so that the latch on the holder engaged with the magazine. With ammunition in place, firing the gun was a simple process. The cocking handle was gripped with the right hand, drawn back to its fullest extent, then pushed forward as the bolt stripped out and chambered the first round. Then the gun could be fired, pulling on the top section of the trigger for single shots, and the bottom section for full-auto.

The firing sequence for the MG 42 was broadly similar to that of the MG 34, with the exception that the MG 42 was generally loaded with the bolt cocked and held to the rear before the belt was inserted into the feed block, either pulling the belt through via a starter tab or, again, opening the top cover and placing the first round against the cartridge stops on the feed tray. Then the safety was disengaged, the gun mounted in the shoulder, and the trigger squeezed to fire. Note that there was no provision for single shots, which could only be achieved by deft trigger technique or by only loading alternate links with cartridges. (The latter procedure meant that the gun had to be recocked after each round was fired, however.)

What really helped the MG 42 become one of the most versatile machine guns in history was its lightning-fast barrel-change system. To change the barrel, all that was required was to push the barrel-change door, located on the right side of the gun just in front of the trigger, forward with the palm of the right hand. This action caused the barrel to pop out from its housing through the right of the barrel jacket, exposing the rear end of the barrel extension. This extension was then gripped in the hand (using a special asbestos cloth to protect against the barrel heat) and the entire

**Barrel-changing in combat, Aachen 1944** (previous pages)

Here we see two Waffen-SS MG 42 teams under fire from US troops in the town of Aachen, Germany, in October 1944. The two men on the left are in the middle of a vulnerable moment – changing the barrel of the MG 42. The barrel currently in the gun has been pushed to its physical limit, hence the red glow, and the gunner is removing it through the barrel door with a cloth – the regulation asbestos *Handschützer* (hot barrel pad) designed specifically for this job was often lost in combat. The assistant gunner has a new barrel held at the ready, which he has just taken from a *Laufschützer* barrel container, which held a single barrel. In the hands of a competent machine-gun crew, the barrel change could be performed in a matter of seconds, but the momentary stop in fire could provide a window of opportunity for attacking infantry to close up. To the right, another MG 42 machine-gunner and his assistant redeploy to a different position. The assistant machine-gunner is carrying two ammunition cans, and on his back he has the Laufbehälte 42 twin barrel container.

Two Nazi volunteers from Turkistan wait for Allied forces with their MG 42. The man on the ground rests his arm on the pads of the Lafette's front leg; these were designed to rest against a man's back when he was carrying the folded tripod. (Cody Images)

barrel could then be withdrawn from the housing. A new barrel was then simply inserted through the barrel-change door and pushed as far as possible to the front, and the barrel extension was pushed about half way into the receiver. Finally, the barrel-change door was swung shut, this action locking the barrel into place. The MG 42 was now ready to use again. A barrel change, performed by a competent two-man team, could be performed in about 4–7 seconds, meaning that in dire straits there would be only a brief drop in the squad firepower when a barrel needed replacing.

This is the mechanical description of firing the MG 34 and MG 42, but what was it like as a physical experience? It very much depended upon what type of mount was used, but in terms of standard bipod use the sensations of firing the gun often depended on the skill of the user. The primary challenge was to keep the gun on target during bursts of automatic fire. A German LMG training manual emphasized the importance of the correct grip during both training and combat:

> The results of the fire will largely depend upon how the machine gun is being held by the machine-gunner. The bipod, elbows and shoulders are the support for the machine gun and they may equal the mount for a heavy machine gun if utilized correctly. Good results may be achieved by digging the points of the boots into the ground for added support… In a normal prone position, the machine-gunner's body must lie directly behind the weapon. The bipod, shoulders and elbows must work together and support the machine gun equally. The weight of the body should press lightly against the bipod. (Quoted in Myrvang 2002: 320)

The manual emphasizes some of the problems that can emerge from a poor grip. If the gun is held too loosely, for example, the rounds will frequently strike the area between the machine-gun position and the target. Too much forward pressure against the bipod, or the body's misalignment with the axis of the gun, and the muzzle would stray up and to the right or left.

Training for both the MG 34 and MG 42 also included some instruction in firing the machine gun from the 'assault position', which basically meant from the hip. The stock of the machine gun was gripped between the bicep and the side of the body, with the front hand reaching forward and gripping the bottom of the bipod legs (in their collapsed position). A further support came from twisting the machine gun's sling around the pistol grip, the sling then looping tightly around the shoulder and neck. Firing the MG 34 and MG 42 from this position took great upper-body strength and diligent trigger control, as the gun could easily swing off target after only a few rounds were fired, endangering your own side in fast-moving combat. An alternative method of fast-mounting the MG 34 or MG 42, at least as seen in photographs, was to rest the barrel jacket on the shoulder of a willing comrade. The experience of being a human mount for a gun like the MG 42 must have been both alarming and truly deafening, and it was probably a last recourse in dire circumstances, or when the gunner required an elevation that his bipod was unable to provide.

In terms of the actual firing sensations and issues of controllability of the two weapons, a useful source is actually the US Army. In January 1944, the US Army produced another of its *Tactical and Technical Trends* reports, this time based on tests of German small arms. Regarding the MG 42, it stated the following:

> A German source states that the MG-42 has a close and dense cone of fire which results in greatly improved observation. The cone of fire has

Only for the brave. This manual-taught method of mounting and firing the MG 34 placed the man at the front under appalling noise and blast from the muzzle. This MG 34 is fed from a Gurttrommel 34 belt drum. (Cody Images)

a slight 'creep' hence this machine gun can be held on the target for only a short time compared with the slower-firing machine guns. This German source states that as a result of the increase in the rate of fire from 420 rpm with the MG-08, to 900 rpm with the MG-34 and to 1,500 rpm with the MG-42, an increase in the percentage of hits in proportion to the length of burst should be obtained. However, preliminary trials in this country have not produced a rate of fire above 1,200 rpm. It would appear, in any case, that a high degree of skill and training are required to obtain the best results from the MG-42 …

a. When Used As a Light Machine Gun
Trials under battle conditions have shown that the best results are obtained from bursts of 5 to 7 rounds, as it is not possible to keep the gun on the target for a longer period. The destruction of the target is therefore accomplished with bursts of 5 to 7 rounds, the point of aim being continually checked. It is of course important that re-aiming should be carried out rapidly, so that the bursts follow one another in quick succession. Under battle conditions the firer can get off approximately 22 bursts in a minute, or approximately 154 rounds. Comparative trials under the same conditions with the MG-34 showed that the best results in this case were obtained with 15 bursts in the minute, each of 7 to 10 rounds, i.e. approximately 150 rounds. It will be seen from this that the ammunition expenditure of the MG-42 is a little higher than with the MG-34, but to balance this, the results on the target with the MG-42 are increased up to approximately 40%. (US Army 1944a)

The results of the US military tests are enlightening, and several key points emerge. The first is how the cyclical rate of fire of each of the weapons

US and German troops train together with the MG3 on Operation *Bright Star* in Egypt in 2001. They are using the shoulder as a mount, a useful if deafening method of giving the gun elevation and rapid deployment. (Cody Images)

affects the practical rate of fire. In the American opinion, the faster-firing MG 42 requires controlled bursts of 5–7 rounds to be most effective, while the MG 34 had optimal bursts of 7–10 rounds. The result is that the practical rate of fire for each weapon, for one minute, is almost the same, although there is the implication that if the MG 42 can be held on target, it will destroy that target more effectively and quickly. Yet we know that the United States was far more reticent about giving the infantry weapons that fired faster than about 500–600rpm, being particularly worried about greedy ammunition consumption. German Army doctrine advocated faster-firing weapons, and their machine-gunners would have delivered controlled bursts of up to a second in duration (in the bipod-mounted LMG role), each burst delivering some 20 rounds on the target.

The report acknowledges, however, that firing the MG 42 requires a measure of extra skill not required in the earlier weapon. The MG 34 delivered a slightly more forgiving experience than the MG 42, on account of its slower rate of fire and heavier build quality. The MG 42, conversely, produced aggressive recoil and shake when fired in lengthy bursts, and would quickly wander off target if not controlled tightly. The muzzle blast would also, in dry conditions, kick up a dust cloud, while the muzzle flash could be dazzling in low-light or night-time conditions.

The challenges of firing the MG 42 come across in several first-hand accounts. One of the most dramatic comes from Guy Sajer's monumental work *The Forgotten Soldier*, a personal history of his time serving as an infantryman on the Eastern Front. Here he describes the opening of a battle around Belgorod in the summer of 1943, in which he is serving as an assistant

These Waffen-SS soldiers on the *Westwall* have a Lafette-mounted MG 34 guarding a stretch of road. Note how low the muzzle of the gun is to the ground – Allied soldiers under fire would often have little idea where the rounds were coming from. (Cody Images)

machine-gunner on what is likely to be an MG 42. The German forces are readying themselves to launch an attack, and Sajer tries to control his nerves in a position only about 100m from an advanced Soviet trench. Note that the translator has used the common Allied term 'Spandau' for the MG 42:

> Suddenly I began to shake uncontrollably [...] I tried shifting my weight, but nothing did any good. I managed to open the magazine [the top cover] and nervously slipped the first belt into the breech of the gun, which the veteran held open for me, and left partly open, to prevent the sound of its clicking shut. [...]
>
> Hals had just opened fire. The veteran slammed our gun shut and fitted it into the hollow of his shoulder.
>
> 'Fire!' shouted the noncom. 'Wipe them out!'
>
> The Russians ran to take their places. The string of 7.7 [sic] cartridges slid through our hands with brutal rapidity, while the noise of the gun burst against our eardrums.
>
> I could see what was happening only with the greatest difficulty. The spandau was shuddering and jumping on its legs, and shaking the veteran, who kept trying to steady himself. Its percussive bark put a final touch on the vast din which had broken out. Through the vibrations and smoke, we were able to observe the horrible impact of our projectiles. (Sajer 1977: 225–26)

This account suggests something of the kicking chaos of firing an MG 42, with the gunner straining to keep the weapon on target, despite being a veteran. Observation of the target is also a problem through the dust, smoke and vibrations, plus the noise levels of the weapon are evidently painful.

Note that the refinements of post-war weapons haven't significantly changed the experience of firing the MG 42. Soldiers of the US 170th Infantry Brigade Combat Team serving in Afghanistan in 2011 had the opportunity to liaise with MG3-equipped German units, who gave the American troops the chance to acquire the *Schützenschnur*, the German infantry's marksmanship badge. For this the US troops had to qualify on three weapons: the HK 9mm pistol, the HK G36 rifle, and the MG3. The sensations of firing the MG3 confirm Sajer's far earlier experience:

> Soldiers fired three, 15-round belts behind the German machine gun. Many soldiers experienced difficulties controlling and firing the German machine gun as the weapon "kicked like a mule," said Spc. Andrew Hamlin, a Stayton, Ore., native, now a military truck driver with Headquarters and Headquarters Company, 2-18th Infantry Battalion. Soldiers twisted and jerked, trying to keep the weapon in the sockets of their shoulders. (Burney 2011: 6)

It seems that neither time nor technology has made the MG 42 derivatives any less forgiving to fire. This having been said, used with the proper tactical mindset (see below) and the right mounts, both the MG 34 and the MG 42's fast rates of fire were far from a disadvantage.

A close-up of the MG3. Note the spare bolt in a pouch on the centre of the table; the rollers that delay the recoil of the bolt are clearly visible in the head. (KrisfromGermany)

## THE LMG ROLE

The German Army built the MG 34 and MG 42 into the core of its infantry organization, right down to the *Gruppe* (squad) level. Until combat losses skewed its proportions, the basic German wartime *Gruppe* consisted of ten men, armed and equipped as follows:

| Soldier | Weapons and equipment | Role |
|---|---|---|
| Group leader | MP 38 or MP 40 submachine gun with six magazines; binoculars; wire cutters; compass; whistle; sunglasses; flashlight | Provide tactical guidance for the group, including directing the emplacement and fire of the machine gun |
| Rifleman 1 (machine-gunner) | MG 34 or MG 42 machine gun; belt drum plus 50 rounds; pistol; gunner's pouch; entrenching tool; flashlight | Responsible for use and maintenance of the machine gun |
| Rifleman 2 (assistant machine-gunner) | Spare machine-gun barrel; four 50-round belt drums; one 300-round ammunition can; pistol; entrenching tool | Provide assistance to Rifleman 1, including supplying ammunition, helping with ammunition feed, emplacing the gun, and providing close protection to the machine-gunner |
| Rifleman 3 (ammunition carrier) | Spare barrel; two 300-round ammunition cans; pistol; entrenching tool | Provide assistance, ammunition supply and close protection to Riflemen 1 and 2 |
| Riflemen 4–9 | Mauser Kar 98k rifle; hand grenades; entrenching tool; extra machine-gun ammunition; anti-aircraft tripod for the machine gun | Combat duties, plus support to the machine-gun team when necessary |

## Combat handling

Watching ammunition consumption was of central importance to any machine-gunner on an active battlefield, but especially those armed with the MG 34 and MG 42. The 1,800 rounds carried by a full squad could be burned through in little more than 10 or 15 minutes of intensive firing. The MG 42 was a particularly hungry gun, and even the most restrained gunner could find himself running worryingly low on ammunition, especially when facing some of the massed Soviet infantry assaults on the Eastern Front, as one old soldier here testifies:

> Rather than simply attacking another section of the defensive rim, or retreating – as I believe any sane commander would do – the Russians continued to send countless troops to attack this one section of the line. They fired mortars into our rank, killing several paratroopers. German machine-gun crews were desperately screaming for ammunition as they continued mowing down groups of Russian infantrymen. They fired their MG 42s in one-second bursts, as they had been trained, but this was not enough to conserve their ammunition. The Russians were very numerous. (Erenberger 2000: 287)

It was in the interests of the rest of the rifle squad to keep their support weapon well-stocked with ammunition. If the machine gun ran silent, the chances of their being overrun increased exponentially.

Another key responsibility of using the MG 34 and MG 42 in combat was to keep the weapons extremely clean. The MG 34 in particular, with its finer tolerances and more complicated mechanism, was especially prone to jamming if not kept spotlessly clean. This proved hard to achieve in the

An MG 42 machine-gunner and the crew of what appears to be a PaK 40 anti-tank gun ready themselves for the defence of the Western Front in 1944. Machine guns and anti-tank weapons often worked in close alliance, the former protecting the latter from infantry assault. (Cody Images)

sand, dust, dirt or snow of theatres such as North Africa, Italy and the Eastern Front. In North Africa, for example, sand and grit would build up in feed mechanisms and actions, leading to improperly chambered cartridges or jammed bolts. Oil, if applied excessively, would combine with sand to form an abrasive grinding paste in the working parts. The MG 42 also had to be cleaned properly and regularly, but its bolt system was generally more tolerant of the ingress of foreign matter, hence its popularity grew rapidly after it was first introduced into combat in North Africa in 1942.

There were general precautions a machine-gunner could take to stop dirt and dust building up in his gun. Both the MG 34 and the MG 42 had hinged dust covers over the ejection ports; the covers popped open automatically when the gun was fired, but the machine-gunner had to ensure that they were closed for most of the time, to prevent dirt entering the receiver through the open port. A fabric dust bag was also available to place over the muzzle to prevent dirt from entering the barrel, although this item is rarely seen in practical use in many photographs. Every gun of course came with a cleaning kit, which included items such as barrel wicks, a pull-through chain, several types of cleaning brush, a chamber cleaner and an oil can. Oiling always had to be kept to a bare minimum, and was even omitted at times.

The sub-zero conditions of the Eastern Front put German machine-gunners on a steep learning curve in acquiring the techniques of keeping the guns working amidst snow and ice, and when the thermometer's needle dropped down to below −20°C. Problems with the MG 34, then the standard machine gun, began even before those temperatures, and delicate metal parts (particularly firing pins) became more brittle and often broke under hard use. Below −20°C, the standard German lubricating and cleaning oils froze, adding to the problems of water getting into the mechanisms and freezing. In a perilous state, with their small arms almost unusable (the problems affected rifles and submachine guns as well as

Two Flemish Waffen-SS soldiers load a belt of 7.92mm rounds into an MG 34. Tracers would constitute roughly one in four of the rounds, the others being standard ball or armour-piercing. (Cody Images)

One of many winter adaptations for the MG 34 and MG 42 was a special snow shoe for the bipod, which prevented the bipod slipping on snow during bursts of automatic fire. (Cody Images)

heavier weapons), many German squads were forced to defend themselves against Russian attacks purely with hand grenades.

In September 1944, with the lessons of several Soviet winters behind them, the German Army released a *Training Manual for the MG 42 as a Light and Heavy Machine Gun (Weapon Training)*, which included a detailed section on the 'Maintenance and Handling of the MG-Weapons in Winter'. Although the booklet was aimed specifically at the MG 42, its lessons would have been readily applicable to the MG 34. The first part of the section gives advice on cleaning, which was to be performed every day. It starts by noting that the machine gun should only be cleaned when it effectively reaches room temperature, or at least when the condensation, caused by bringing the cold gun into a warm room, has disappeared.

Occasionally, gun parts would freeze solid in wet, icy conditions, and the manual urges the operator not to attempt to clear these problems with brute force, but to de-ice the gun gently with indirect heat and by using kerosene. While the outer parts of the gun could be oiled, the manual recommended that: 'The internal, moving parts of the machine gun must be kept dry, clean and without oil. When the machine gun is fired and becomes warm, it can then be oiled in a pause in the shooting.' (OKH 1944: I: 54.2) However, the manual also acknowledges that the soldier can manufacture a 'frost proof' oil by mixing standard oils in a 1:2 ratio of kerosene/oil, making an oil that resisted freezing in temperatures as low as −40°C. (This trick of mixing oil and kerosene had been picked up from the Soviets.) In terms of general storage of the MG 42, the manual stated that 'the machine gun is to be stored at the temperature that it will be shot' (I: 54.2), although the gun had to be kept in a specific storage enclosure that protected it against cold, snow and damp. The muzzle and other exposed parts were to be wrapped in *Zeltbahn* shelter-quarter cloths or purpose-specific covers to shield against the ingress of snow, ice and other debris.

An additional point to come out of the 1944 guide was a distinct warning against placing hot barrels in the snow to cool off. Doing so could

Exhausted German infantry take a break from operations on the Eastern Front. An MG 34 stands by on its bipod, ready loaded in case of an emergency. (Cody Images)

result in the barrel warping due to the extremely sudden temperature change, after which it would become useless.

Much of our study of MG 34 and MG 42 use has so far applied to the guns in their LMG format, used straight from the bipod. Yet both guns were capable of far more varied roles, which added to their battlefield effect at every level.

## THE MMG/HMG ROLES

The genius of the MG 34 and MG 42 lay only partly in the design of the gun itself. Equal vision was applied to the design of both its sights and its mounts, which had the capacity to change both the gun's function and its capacity for

### MG 34 teams near Moscow, December 1941 (previous pages)

A German Army machine-gun team fires their tripod-mounted MG 34 from a prepared defensive position on the outskirts of Moscow, December 1941. Their MG 34 is mounted on the Lafette 34 tripod, while the gunner takes aim through the MG *Zieleinrichtung* optical sight. Used for indirect fire in this mode, the MG 34 had a maximum range of up to 3,500m; the squad leader on the left observes the target area through his binoculars. Ammunition consumption in combat could be extremely high – as indicated by the two 300-round *Patronenkasten* ammunition cans on the trench lip, and the pile of spent shell casings – and a spare barrel is kept ready in its container to the gunner's right side. Behind them, another machine-gun group runs up in support. The machine-gunner of this group carries a 50-round belt as well as the MG 34, while the rifleman next to him has two 300-round ammunition cans. The MP 40-armed squad leader is carrying a spare barrel container on his back; normally the assistant machine-gunner and one of the other riflemen would carry spare barrels, but the effect of casualties on the squad meant that everyone had to fall into supporting roles to keep the machine gun functioning.

destruction. Fitting an optical sight alone enabled the guns to deliver direct fire out to 3,000m, but combining optical sights plus a tripod carriage meant the gun could deliver indirect fire to 3,500m, and in more extended bursts of fire than could be achieved with the bipod-mounted gun. Before looking at the tactical arrangements of the MG 34 and MG 42 in MMG/HMG roles, we need to get to grips with the mounts and sights available.

Winter conditions presented a formidable challenge to a machine-gun team, as suggested here. The key problem was preventing the gun's moving parts freezing solid in icy conditions, a skill that required careful gun-oiling procedures and correct storage. (Cody Images)

## Tripod mounts and optical sights

The Lafette 34 and Lafette 42 tripod mounts were the essential counterparts to the guns' integral bipods. The differences between the two are actually fairly minimal, and revolve around the systems of actually mounting the gun to the tripod cradle. The basic Lafette mount weighed in at 20kg, and could be set up in one of three heights, designated as 'high', 'kneeling' and 'prone'. This flexibility in height setting was appreciated on the battlefield, as it meant that even when using the tripod, a machine-gun team could get close to the ground, or hunkered well down in a machine-gun position. The front and rear legs of the mount were adjustable, and scales on the rear legs allowed the gun to be collapsed, picked up and moved between positions but set up to the same height configuration straightaway. The two thick leather *Polsters* (pads) seen attached to the front leg were used when the tripod was collapsed and being carried; the pads rested against the carrier's back.

As explained above, the Lafette was a softmount type – the gun cradle was attached to powerful recoil springs, meaning the recoil was soaked up in a controlled fashion, which combined with the rigidity of the tripod meant the gun stayed on target even during bursts of sustained fire.

A *Zielfernrohrhalter* (optical sight bracket) was provided on the left-hand upper part of the mount, and it would take one of several kinds of optical sight available. Yet the Lafette not only improved accuracy through its sighting options and recoil control, but also through mechanisms for fine-tuning fire control. The front of the mount was pivoted to allow gun traverse, and the extent of the traverse left and right could be fixed by use of adjustable traverse stops. Elevation was manually performed by a handwheel, but at the rear of the mount was also the *Einstellring für Tiefenfeuer* (searching-fire unit). This unit, when activated, mechanically controlled the rise and fall of the gun, elevating the gun for five rounds then depressing it for four rounds. The effect at the target of this system was to lengthen the 'beaten zone', a roughly oval area of bullet impacts created by the 'cone of fire' comprising the totality of bullet trajectories from muzzle to target. In short, the device spread the destruction over a wider area. Machine-gunners would have learnt, through both tabular information and experience, how much adjusting the traverse or searching-fire settings would relate to the impact of the bullets hundreds of metres beyond the muzzle. For example, to deliver a 100m beaten zone at 1,200m, the searching-fire unit was set to number 1, whereas to deliver the same beaten zone at 3,300m it was set to number 5.

Attached to the searching-fire unit was the mount's trigger handle, which enabled the user to fire the gun without affecting the stability of the gun's point of aim. On the MG 34 it could be adjusted for both single-shot and full-automatic fire as necessary, although some simplified late-war mounts had the trigger configured for full-auto fire only.

Of course, the mount was only part of the equation for turning an MG 34 or MG 42 into an MMG or HMG. Optical sights were also essential to delivering long-range direct or indirect fire accurately. The first optical sight introduced specifically for mounting on the MG Lafette was the

A three-man team adjusts the aim of an MG 34 on its Lafette 34 mount. The gunner is looking through the MG Z optical sight, the standard optical sight on the MG 34. (Cody Images)

**US War Department information of elevation and traverse of Lafette 34**

(4) ELEVATION AND TRAVERSE.

(a) The front end of the cradle is carried on a swivel mounting at the junction of the three tripod legs, while the rear end is supported by the elevating gear. The front leg is telescopically adjustable, and is provided with a clamping lever for fixing the telescopic parts after they have been adjusted. A traversing arc, on which the elevating gear is carried by a traversing slide, acts as a brace between the two rear legs which are jointed, each joint being fitted with a clamping wing nut. An adjustable center stay provided with a clamping lever is connected between the traversing arc and the front leg.

(b) Elevation is adjusted by a handwheel on the left of the elevating gear, while adjustments for line are made by shifting the traversing slide along the traversing arc by means of a handle on the right, in which an oil bottle is fitted. A wing nut is provided for clamping the elevating gear and a clamping lever for locking the traversing slide. Adjustable elevating and traversing stops are also provided to enable the gun to be elevated and traversed between predetermined limits. The traversing stops are arranged for the traverse arc, which is graduated to facilitate adjustment of the stops (fig. 36).

(c) In front of the elevating gear is an automatic searching fire device, operated by the recoil of the gun in the cradle, which causes a projection on the cradle slide to strike a roller on the device. Actuated in this manner, the device alternately elevates the cradle step by step, and depresses it similarly each time a shot is fired. The limits of the searching fire, and consequently the distance on the ground covered by it, can be increased or reduced by means of a graduated setting ring. (US War Dept 1943: 26, 31)

MG Z, introduced around 1937. (Older MG 08 optical sights were used before production of the MG Z had caught up with demand.) Later wartime models included the MG Z 40, which could be used with both the MG 34 and MG 42, and the late-war MG Z 44, which was designed for direct-fire only, with improved magnification over previous optical sights. Note that the MG Z and MG Z 40 could both be used with the wartime *Vorsatzfernrohr MG Zieleinrichtung* (MG Periscope Accessory), introduced in late 1942. Using optical sights meant that the gunner had to position his eye above the line of the mount, the result being he ran the risk – often realized in the first years of the war – of being shot in the head by an enemy sniper or counter-machine-gun fire. The periscope attachment meant that the gunner could use the optical sight from a behind-cover position.

## Heavy fire

Using the optical sights effectively for indirect fire was a complicated business, requiring a highly technical understanding of the sight's traverse and elevation settings and their relation to various range tables and ancillary range-calculating equipment. Training and practice made the process familiar, however, and German gunners were noted for their ability to use a group of tripod-mounted machine guns to saturate a target area from distance. With about 13 machine guns in its complement, a German infantry company could send out well over 2,000 rounds every minute against enemy formations. (The company's firepower could be increased by the allocation of weapons from the battalion's Machine Gun Company, which consisted of three HMG platoons.) Allied troops forming up for an attack were particularly vulnerable; the first they would know of the enemy machine guns would be the crack of rounds splitting the air, observed bullet impacts and soldiers dropped to the floor, dead or wounded. The only counter to such fire would be to return machine-gun, mortar or artillery fire rapidly, if the location of the guns could be identified.

Numerous Allied reports from the advance across Normandy and France in 1944 speak of being caught in German machine-gun crossfire, with entire battalions and even divisions unable to make significant headway against scything fire. One such report, from the US 329th Infantry on 8 August 1944, concerns the division's first contact with the Germans on 4 July 1944, and outlines the reasons for the high casualties:

> a. DATA: First Engagement
> > (1) Initial date contacted enemy – 4 July 1944
> > (2) Organization that initially contacted enemy – 2nd Battalion, 329th Infantry
> > (3) Casualties – Companies E & F, 2nd Battalion, approximately 35% casualties. Company E, 2 KIA, 37 WIA, 40 MIA. Company F, 6 KIA, 27 WIA, 20 MIA.
> > (4) Principal enemy weapons – Enemy had full use of heavy machine guns with excellent displacement with maximum field of fire. Mortars and 88 mm guns were used extensively in some sectors.
> > (5) Location – Le Plessis, Normandy, France (US Army 1944c: 2)

We saw earlier, in the context of urban fighting, how the Germans were masters of placing machine guns in mutually supportive relationships.

Waffen-SS armoured vehicle crewmen in action. The man on the left is firing a Soviet PPSh-41 submachine gun, while his comrade is loading a Patronentrommel 34 double drum magazine, his hand through the magazine's top strap. (Cody Images)

Such is hinted at in the phrase 'excellent displacement with maximum field of fire', as a core reason why the day's casualties were so high. (The report also noted that the US soldiers' own lack of combat experience contributed to the heavy losses.) In another action, one US technical sergeant noted that during one US attack against a German position 'the Germans had at least two platoons with two MG-42s each, with at least three in our sector. We keep going forward and we keep losing people. They just decimated us.' Other American troops talk of their companies being caught in the frenzied buzzing of thousands of rounds cutting through the air, and seeing their unit torn apart in a matter of minutes by the storm of fire. MG 42s also killed or wounded hundreds of US troops who poured onto Omaha Beach on 6 June 1944 – multiple guns were positioned along the coast so that they could fire along the beach, parallel to the shoreline, catching the landing US soldiers in appalling enfilading fire. What is certain is that many thousands of Allied troops, on all fronts, fell victim to rounds fired from machine guns whose report they did not even hear.

A squad leader scans the horizon for enemy activity, while his MG 34 crew await instructions. Mounted on the Lafette tripod, the MG 34 had an indirect-fire range of up to 3,500m. (Cody Images)

**US Army report on MG 42 in medium machine-gun role**

Long periods of sustained fire must definitely be avoided, as they do not produce the best results and lead to an unwarranted expenditure of ammunition. The reasons for this being, first, if the extraordinarily dense cone of fire of the MG-42 is on the target, then this should be destroyed in approximately 50 rounds; secondly, if the cone of fire is not on the target then the gun must be re-aimed, if necessary with adjustments to the sight. In order to assess the position of the cone of fire, fire must not be opened until an observation has been obtained.

For instance, if with a range of 2,000 yards the time of flight is 4.7 seconds, then a useful observation cannot be obtained in less than six seconds. Sustained fire for a period of six seconds, however, is the equivalent of an ammunition expenditure of 150 rounds, whereas an observation of the position of the cone of fire or of the effects on the target, could have been obtained with 50 rounds.

Trials under battle conditions on the same lines as those carried out in action with the MG-34 have shown that, in general, when using the MG-42 as a medium machine gun, bursts of 50 rounds with repeated checking of the point of aim give the best results.

In this way, not only will the best results on the target be achieved, but the expenditure of ammunition will be kept within limits which will be very little in excess of expenditure with the earlier MGs. (US Army 1944)

## Anti-aircraft mounts

The fast rates of fire, and long reach, of the MG 34 and MG 42 made them both suited to use as AA weapons. The MG Lafette had further versatility through the *Lafettenaufsatzstück* (Lafette AA Extension Unit), essentially a long extension tube that fitted to the top of the tripod with a mount for the gun. This was an equally popular alternative to the dedicated AA tripods, the Dreibein 34 and Dreibein 40. These were largely based on the old AA mounts for the MG 08, and they were made either from aluminium, a

A twin MG 34 AA mount. Both guns are fitted with the *Panzermantel* heavy barrel jacket, more typically seen on MG 34s fitted to armoured vehicles. Sighting is through a simple ring sight and bead. (Cody Images)

magnesium/aluminium alloy or steel. Photographs show the Dreibein mounts used in a variety of contexts, not just for air defence but also for guard duty over key positions, in which it was preferable for the machine-gunner to remain standing. The main limitation of these mounts was that the elevation made belt feed problematic – the weight of a long hanging belt was too much for an MG 34 or MG 42 to pull through under its own steam, unless well-supported by an assistant machine-gunner. Hence the AA-mounted guns tend to be seen with box magazines or with man-supported belts.

There were also a range of vehicle AA mounts for the MG 34 and MG 42. The most basic was the Fliegerdrehstütze 36 (Anti-Aircraft Pedestal Mount 36), which combined the Lafette's AA extension tube with the Dreibein mount. A gear crank system allowed the operator to elevate or lower the central tube to meet his body requirements. The Fliegerdrehstütze 36 was commonly seen mounted on trucks, train cars

The German Fallschirmjäger here are firing the MG 34 from the Dreibein 34 AA tripod. The MG 34 had a mount for an AA ring sight along the front jacket. (Cody Images)

and other open vehicles. A far more developed AA mount, however, was the Zwillingsockel 36, specifically for the MG 34. This was a dual machine-gun mount, the only adaptation to the guns being the removal of their stocks. The mount could rotate through 360 degrees, the motive power coming from the operator's legs – he occupied a seat connected to the mount – while a brake lever could be applied to stop rotation. Both guns were sighted using a central AA ring sight, and feed for each gun was via Patronenkasten 36 150-round ammunition boxes.

The Zwillingsockel 36 could be mounted to vehicle platform, such as the bed of a truck, or to the unusual MG-Wagen 36. This latter mobile AA platform consisted of a two-wheeled cart containing the machine guns and their operator (the floor of the cart was ridged to enable the gunner to gain grip while traversing the mount), plus related equipment and ammunition. When not emplaced on its own, the machine-gun wagon was pulled by two horses, a limber cart connected between the horses and the wagon and seated the driver and machine-gun group leader. (It also contained items such as spares for the machine guns and fodder for the horses.) To modern eyes, the MG-Wagen 36 appears as something of an oddity. But with a combined cyclical rate of some 1,800rpm, the system was certainly capable of giving an Allied aircraft cause for concern if it passed within 1,000m of the barrels (the official effective range of the MG 34 and MG 42 in AA use). Note that there was a version of the Zwillingsockel 36 for the MG 42, called the Zwillingsockel 42, although the photographic evidence of this being in widespread use is limited.

One real curiosity in the world of MG 34 mounts was the gun's application as an armament for assault gliders, specifically the LS-DFS 230 glider. The gun was mounted on the fuselage, just beneath the right side of the cockpit, and it was boresighted so that its aiming point corresponded with that of a small ring sight mounted on the windscreen in front of the pilot. To operate the gun when the aircraft was airborne, one of the passengers in the rear compartment placed his hand through a zippered opening in the fuselage and fired the gun conventionally using the pistol grip. (The conventional layout and operation of the gun meant that the soldiers inside the glider could take the gun with them after landing.) The pilot shouted the commands 'Fire' and 'Cease Fire' at the opportune moments. As a means of air defence against enemy aircraft, the glider-mounted MG 34 had limited utility. It probably had more practical purpose in giving bursts of fire against enemy ground troops at a 'hot' landing zone.

## Armoured use

It is worth bearing in mind that although the MG 42 has become the more historically prominent of the German universal machine guns, the MG 34 actually had the wider distribution. Partly this is on account of the longer period of production enjoyed by the MG 34 before the introduction of its successor, but it is also due to the MG 34's widespread use as a vehicular

A German *Gruppe* marches past a knocked-out Elefant assault gun. While the gunner is equipped with the MG 42, an MG 34 is visible projecting from the Elefant's full hull, set in a *Kugelblende* ball mount. (Cody Images)

defence weapon. The MG 42 was itself used from vehicles, as we have seen, but its barrel-change system made it unsuited to enclosed mounts, such as those necessary for coaxial machine guns. It remained arguably the superior gun for LMG use, and in some HMG settings. Furthermore, the MG 34's sensitivity to jamming angered many, including Oberst Kuhn, commander of 3rd Panzer Brigade in the West in 1940, who stated in an after-action report: 'In operations against motorized infantry, tanks have proven to demonstrate complete superiority. As long as there was no threat from anti-tank weapons, the enemy infantry was shot to pieces by them. The drum magazine and fixed mount of the MG 34 caused constant stoppages – it is not a suitable weapon for war.' (Quoted in Hartman 2010: 147–48)

Despite such reservations, not everyone warmed to the MG 42's voracious appetite for 7.92mm ammunition; and the MG 34 had feed options (such as the drum magazine) that were more suited to internal vehicle use, even if they didn't necessarily contribute to reliability.

A particularly unusual transport mount for the MG 34 was that designed for a military bicycle. The gun could be fixed to the frame of an Army-issue bicycle, with the stock by the pedals, the barrel running up past the handlebars and the muzzle sitting high above the front wheel.

German troops dressed in winter smocks struggle through the snows of the Ardennes in late 1944. The motorcycle sidecar is fitted with an MG 42 on a flexible mount. So configured, such weapons were typically fitted with a 50-round *Gurttrommel* belt drum. (Cody Images)

Two 75-round magazines or 300-round ammunition cans could be stored over the rear wheel. While looking slightly comical to modern eyes, this means of transportation could be briskly effective, as bicycle-mounted troops were capable of travelling at twice the speed of foot-sloggers on roads or smooth tracks.

For combat use, the MG 34 capitalized on an extremely flexible variety of mounts. It was seen fitted to the sidecars of motorcycle and sidecar combinations. The humble Kübelwagen light vehicle could take the gun either via a simple pedestal mount or a special spring-stabilized arm mount, which improved the gunner's ability to track and fire on targets while the vehicle was moving. Hefty amounts of ammunition could be stored on the vehicle's rear deck, turning a Kübelwagen into a substantial mobile-fire platform.

The MG 34's potential as a vehicular machine gun was realized in armoured vehicles, either as primary or secondary armament. Before the MG 34 was introduced, the MG 13 was the main tanker machine gun of the German Army, but the MG 34's superior qualities soon won through. Mounts included twin-gun turret mounts such as those used in the PzKpfw I tank (which was exclusively machine-gun armed), plus flexible hull *Kugelblende* (ball mounts) on cannon-armed tanks.

Ball-mounted MG 34s worked under tight limitations. Vision either side of the mount was poor – in the region of 15 degrees left or right – and the gun had a very slim range of elevation and traverse. For such reasons, the ball-mounted MG 34 had optical sights zeroed to only 200m, the gun having little application beyond short-range defence against infantry, or possibly reaching out further to deliver ranging tracer fire against enemy armour before engaging with the main gun. Barrel change within the confines of a turret could be a physical challenge, hence in combat it might be the case that a hot barrel was simply discarded, and replaced by one of two spare barrels kept in twin barrel carriers. From February 1941 a heavy steel barrel jacket was also introduced for the MG 34, which had a reduced number of ventilation holes.

The thinking behind the jacket was primarily to make the exterior parts of the gun more resilient to the small-arms fire, explosions and shrapnel that typically raked any armoured vehicle in combat. The revised gun could also be supplied with a 'ground kit' that enabled the tank crew to adapt the gun for bipod-mounted use outside their vehicle. A rotating *Fliegerbeschussgerät* (turret AA mount) for an additional MG 34 provided a tank commander or other crew member with limited air defence.

In the wider inventory of German armoured vehicles, such as half-tracks and tank destroyers, the MG 34 was the principal means of anti-personnel and AA fire. Some utilized the *Fliegerbeschussgerät*, while others fitted a version of the Lafette softmount with a special bracket adaptation for half-tracks. Some assault-gun and tank-destroyer crews also benefited from a remote-control mount, developed in response to heavy casualties among exposed machine-gun crews on open-top armoured vehicles. This system mechanically extended the gun mount and controls into the crew compartment of the vehicle, which allowed the gunner to traverse, elevate, aim (via a periscope) and fire the gun while under cover. Yet the remote mount's 50-round drum magazine was awkward to load, so the system's distribution was insignificant. More broadly, however, some 50,000 tanker MG 34s were produced, providing armoured vehicle crews with more defensive and offensive options than just their main armament.

Although the MG 34 was by far the more common weapon for armoured vehicle use, the MG 42 was also used. Here we see an MG 42 mounted on a half-track, by means of a swing-arm mount. (Cody Images)

## Fortress guns

For all its exposition of manoeuvre warfare, the Wehrmacht was also a very defensively minded organization, particularly as the war turned against Germany from around 1942. Extensive inland and coastal positions emerged like monstrous ferro-concrete sentinels through various stretches of the Third Reich, most visibly in the *Westwall* of western Germany, and the *Atlantikwall* stretching along the coast of Western Europe from Norway to Spain. Other fortress positions were dotted around cities, salient terrain or ports.

Both MG 34s and MG 42s were used as defensive weapon systems in such fortifications, and again, the mount changed the configuration of the weapon and its use. For heavily armoured casemates, in which the gunner would have complete protection, the MG 34 (not the MG 42, again because of its barrel-change system) could be mounted in *Panzernestlaffetten* (armoured loophole mounts). These hefty mounts had the front barrel jacket enclosed by a thick armoured cup, so only the muzzle of the gun projected outside. Aiming was performed via a Panzer Zielfernrohr (PzZF) optical sight mounted above the gun, and the ammunition feed was from a Patronenkasten Pz 34 ammunition can. Both the MG 34 and the MG 42 could be mounted, via different cradle adapters, for pillbox and emplacement use. The mounts used were modified versions of the MG 08 Maxim sledmounts, with softmount recoil control and traverse and elevation controls to deliver precision firepower at a pre-designated killing zone in front of the position.

The devastation that could be wrought by a fortress machine gun was considerable and harrowing. Nowhere was this more appallingly demonstrated than at the infamous Omaha Beach in Normandy on 6 June 1944, during the D-Day landings. In just one of the German emplacements overlooking the beach, Widerstandsnest 62 (Resistance Nest 62), machine-gunner Heinrich Severloh of the 352nd Infantry Division personally gunned down dozens of US soldiers pouring from their landing vessels onto East Red and Fox Green sectors. Severloh's autobiography later

A Lafette-mounted MG 34 in an Atlantic Wall pillbox, France, 1943. The MG 34 was much better suited to fortress use than the MG 42, because its barrel-change system was more convenient for enclosed spaces. (Cody Images)

Armoured trains like this one presented formidable firepower on the Eastern Front, where they were most common. In addition to the heavy guns and AA cannon, MG 34s project from the sides of the cars to provide close-in defence. (Cody Images)

claimed that he had personally killed more than 1,000 US soldiers with his MG 42. While there are major question marks over this figure, there is no doubting that the Omaha Beach machine guns certainly accounted for a high percentage of the 3,000 US casualties taken that day. The devastation of such fire was vividly evoked by Irwin Shaw, a US reporter present on the beach that day: 'Under fire themselves all the way in, the Rangers became prime targets of mortars, the 88 and a torrent of machine-gun fire. The ramps were dropped, exposing the men tightly bunched together to direct automatic fire. Flesh exploded from heavy impacts. For every man it seemed he had reached the last minutes of his life, so minds as well as muscles were paralyzed.' (Quoted in Taylor & Martin 1997: 52) Such accounts remind us, with no room for misunderstanding, that the MG 34 and MG 42 were intentional instruments of mass slaughter, however refined or innovative their engineering.

The MG 34 was fitted on simple AA mounts to Kriegsmarine (German Navy) vessels for basic air defence, including to the conning towers of U-boats. (Cody Images)

# IMPACT
## 'Hitler's Buzzsaw'

The impact of both the MG 34 and MG 42 in World War II was as much psychological as it was physical. Both guns were inaccurately labelled as 'Spandaus' by the Allies, based upon the manufacturer's plate on the MG 42, which referred to the Spandau borough of Berlin. Associated with this name was a notorious type of sound emitted by the ultra-fast-firing MG 42, likened to the sound of linoleum ripping or a buzzsaw cutting through a knot of wood. Captain Alastair Borthwick of 5th Battalion, The Seaforth Highlanders, remembered this auditory signature all too well:

> There was something much too personal about a Spandau. It did not aim at an area: it aimed at you, and its rate of fire was prodigious. It had a vindictive sound. Each burst began with an odd hiccup before getting into its stride, so that the crack of the first round was distinct and all the others ran together like the sound of tearing calico. Their *pup-turrrr, pup-turrrr* was the most distinctive sound on the battlefield … (Quoted in Bull 2005: 19–20)

The sound of the MG 42, plus its slashing effect on its target, also earned the machine gun a variety of epithets and nicknames. The names changed according to the nationality of troops using them, but they had a common thread. For Germans, the MG 42 was the *Hitlersäge* (Hitler's Saw), *Die Schnellespritze* (the Fast Sprayer) or the apt and more literal *Knochensäge* (Bone Saw). A bawdier version was *Die Tripperspritze* (the Gonorrhoea Syringe). British and American troops nicknamed it 'Hitler's Buzzsaw' or 'Hitler's Zipper', while the Soviets termed it the 'Linoleum Ripper'. An account from a soldier of the Canadian 5th Armoured Division on the

Italian Front here explains the origins of some other nicknames for the German machine guns:

> From beyond the embankment came the steady rattle of small arms, mostly the enemy's. It was easy to identify them. Brens could push out a maximum 540 rounds per minute, while the MG 34 delivered eight to nine hundred, [the MG] 42 could spit out twelve hundred. Someone somewhere on the battlefield came up with the term 'rubber gun' for the Jerry MGs – not an apt name, but nonetheless that's what we came to know them [*sic*] until the more descriptive term 'cheese cutter' took over. By whatever name we called it, the Jerry machine-gun was a weapon to be feared. (Scislowski 1997: 123–24)

Beyond the nicknames, there was no doubting the persuasion of the universal machine gun, which would send Allied troops to cover the moment it barked. There was evidently concern among the highest authorities about the effect the MG 34 and MG 42 had on morale, as evidenced by the content of US War Department Film Bulletin F.B. No. 181, produced in 1944 and entitled *Automatic Weapons: American vs. German*. The basic tenor of the film is to convince the US soldier that the German automatic weapon had a 'bark worse than its bite'. Its opening lines acknowledge that the sound of the German guns – specifically the MG 34, the MG 42 and the MP 38/MP 40 submachine guns – is of particular concern to the GI on the battlefield:

German Fallschirmjäger deploy their MG 42 in the rubble of Monte Cassino in 1944. Such weapons imposed a fearful cost on Allied soldiers attacking up the slopes of the mountain. (Cody Images)

These are the weapons we are up against in the European and Mediterranean theaters of operation. But we've captured not only the film, but the actual weapons and ammunition. Just what are they like? How fast and how accurately do they fire compared to our weapons? And most important to you, how do they sound?

[...]

Listen to that ... Fast! That thing sprays a lot of lead. And you're scared, because the German gun fires faster than anything you've run into before. So much faster than the slow steady bark of American machine guns you heard all through training. And you can't see them either – in combat they aren't sitting out in the open.

Against the backdrop of stirring martial music, the film then goes on to attempt to demythologize the German guns one by one. A US squad (of actor soldiers), seen initially pinned down by the German weapons, calmly goes about taking on the enemy, sending some men out to the flanks while others establish a base of fire. 'Nobody seems especially afraid of that gun, nobody except the replacement, who can't get over the fast burp of that German gun.' The film then range tests the German automatic weapons against their US equivalents (the Browning M1917 on a tripod, the Browning M1919 on a bipod and the Thompson .45cal SMG), firing the heavier weapons at man-sized targets 300yd away. As the demonstrators show with scientific satisfaction, the US weapons achieve more hits on the targets every time. The narrator also explains about the MG 42 that 'another thing about that high rate of fire ... it eats up ammunition almost three times as fast as our own machine guns'. He illustrates how German four-gun machine-gun platoons use eight more men than an equivalent US platoon just to carry ammunition, men that the US forces use instead for either an additional machine gun or other infantry power.

Whether such films actually made the front-line infantryman feel better about confronting German weapons is very seriously in doubt. The implicit mockery of German automatic weapons implied in the film was betrayed by actual battlefield experience. The German infantry machine-gun teams were tactically intelligent units, and if their guns had higher rates of fire than the enemy weapons, they were certain to use it to good effect. Note, for example, the view of Lieutenant Sydney Jary of 4th Battalion, The Somerset Light Infantry, fighting in Normandy in 1944: 'The forward platoon ...

An MG 42 team in Kharkov, March 1943. Used from a bipod the MG 42 could usefully command ranges in direct-fire mode up to 2,000m. (Cody Images)

had barely crossed the stream when concentrated Spandau fire came from the front and both flanks. There must have been about twelve machine guns firing at one time. This devastating firepower stopped the battalion dead in its tracks. There was no way forward or around it and no way to retire.' (Quoted in Bull 2005: 15)

One point that the US War Department film scrupulously avoided was the fact that multiple German machine guns could be acting in concert, and with interlocking fields of fire. The result was a terrifying, broad beaten ground through which troops could not advance without incurring serious casualties. Moreover, there was no doubting the terminal results of the 7.92mm round on the human body, especially when delivered with a muzzle velocity of 755m/sec. At relatively short ranges, such as 200m, the rounds would often go straight through the victim and continue their flight. If the bullets began to tumble inside the body, as often occurred in fire delivered at longer ranges, then horrible ragged entry holes or internal injuries would be inflicted, causing death by organ damage and blood volume shock. Tom Renouf, serving with 51st Highland Division in 1944–45, witnessed the grim effects of 'Spandau' impacts at first hand:

> Meanwhile, our platoon secured some high ground further forward, where we came under heavy Spandau fire. A bullet hit our corporal, Sam Clarke from Elphinstone, near Ormiston, in the leg, severing an artery. He died shortly afterwards despite the best efforts of Private Neaves, from Dundee, who tried to stem the flow of blood with his own emergency dressing. This was my first experience of direct Spandau fire. All you heard was a short burst and then people were falling. (Renouf 2011)

Tens of thousands of men around the world at war succumbed to similar grievous injuries, but being behind the gun also brought its fair share of peril.

German troops take cover from small-arms fire behind a PzKpfw 35(t). The MG 34 was a revolution in infantry firepower, giving a small team of infantry the ability to deliver 900rpm firepower. (Cody Images)

## VULNERABLE WARRIORS

We have already noted that being a German machine-gunner brought with it considerable physical and tactical burdens, not least the fact that you became a magnet for the other side's firepower. Being the operator of such impressive firepower did not shield a man from the perils that faced any soldier on the battlefield; the opposite was true in fact. German soldiers operating on the Eastern Front during the victorious early months of Operation *Barbarossa* in 1941 often noted with bewilderment how Soviet troops would just keep attacking in persistent waves, despite the ranks of soldiers being cut down by driving machine-gun fire. At the same time, they would sense that what they delivered could return to them from a powerful enemy. We get this impression from Heinrich Happe, a German medical officer, witnessing the demise of a group of retreating Russians:

> By late afternoon we had pressed the retreating Russians right to the edge of the marshlands, across which the only passage was the bridge of logs. They fled across it, but our heavy machine guns raked the bridge and picked them off at will. As we saw them being mown down, unable to jump either to the right or left to escape the cross-fire, we thought uneasily of our own fate when we reached the other side of the crossing, which was likely to be under equally murderous fire from the Reds. (Happe 1957, quoted in Flower & Reeves 1997: 210)

The German machine-gunners in this incident were not to die that day, but countless others would see their end manning an MG 34 or MG 42. The problem became especially acute in the later years of the war. Despite Herculean efforts from German industry, Germany's weapons factories were never able to compete with the prodigious volume of weapons production achieved by the Allies in the later years of the war. Thus while Germany produced 159,000 artillery pieces between 1939 and 1945, the Allies combined produced 914,600, 516,600 of those from Soviet factories alone. In tanks and self-propelled guns – vehicles against which the MG 34 and MG 42 could deliver nothing more than scratches – Germany made 46,857 while the United States produced 88,410, the USSR 105,251 and the UK 27,896. Disparities in mortar and machine-gun production were even greater. Total German output of mortars was 73,484 units, while for the Allies it was 914,682. And for machine guns, Germany's final wartime figure was 674,280; the Allies made 4,744,484. Even allowing for the drain of the Pacific theatre, it was clear to all by 1944 that the Allies had developed a total superiority in battlefield firepower, never mind the comparable Allied superiority developed in airpower.

This shift in the balance of fire would ultimately limit the impact of the MG 34 and MG 42 during World War II. As we have seen, both machine guns were capable of inflicting very heavy casualties and of forcing large units to a standstill. Without weapons of this capability and flexibility, it is likely that Allied infantry in all theatres would have been able to advance towards their objectives at greater speed and lower cost. These weapons were true force multipliers, enabling a small team of men to put down fire

Gebirgsjäger mountain troops fire an MG 42. This weapon has the older style of slab-sided cocking handle, replaced by a vertical bar that gave better cocking grip. (Cody Images)

that couldn't have been achieved by dozens of riflemen.

Yet once the Allies fully recognized the destructive capability of these two machine guns, they used their heavy firepower where possible to compensate. In the same way that a single insurgent sniper in Afghanistan can be neutralized by an airstrike-delivered precision bomb, German machine-gun teams found themselves hammered by heavier weapons against which they had little recourse. While US infantry took cover from machine-gun fire, their mortars and artillery could reply with bombardments against machine-gun positions, often at ranges even beyond the capabilities of MG 34 and MG 42 indirect fire. Irwin Shaw saw the US mortars in action during the advance through North-West Europe:

Twenty minutes later they had reached the line of hedge from which the enemy machine-guns had been firing. Mortars had finally found the range and had destroyed one of the nests in a corner of the field, and the other sections had pulled out before Noah [one of the US soldiers] and the Company reached them.

Wearily, Noah kneeled by the side of the cleverly concealed, heavily sandbagged position, now blown apart to reveal three Germans dead at their wrecked gun. One of the Germans was still kneeling behind it. (Shaw 1946, quoted in Flower & Reeves 1997: 891)

Many combat accounts of the North-West Europe campaign speak not only of the terror that the German machine guns could inflict on Allied troops, but also the overwhelming firepower that tended to engulf those guns once they could be targeted. Increasingly, German companies would stay in place long enough to hit advancing Allied troops hard with cross-fire, but then pull out when the weight of fire directed against them became overwhelming. General Heinrich von Lüttwitz, the commander of XLVII Panzer Corps, observed that:

The incredibly heavy artillery and mortar fire of the enemy is something new, both for the seasoned veterans of the Eastern Front and the new arrivals from reinforcement units … The average rate of fire on the divisional sector is four thousand artillery rounds and five thousand mortar rounds per day. This is multiplied many times before an enemy attack, however small. For instance, on one occasion when the British made an attack on a sector of only two companies they expended three thousand five hundred rounds in two hours. The Allies are waging war regardless of expense. (Freidlin & Richardson 1956, quoted in Flower & Reeves 1997: 898)

Here was the ultimate limitation of the *Einheitsmaschinengewehr*. The MG 34 and MG 42 were superb tactical weapons, ideally suited for assault, manoeuvre and delivering a base of fire against an infantry enemy. In the end, the relevance of those qualities was subsumed under the sheer, crushing weight of firepower, a blunt instrument to hammer the German forces into submission. Alongside a whole range of technologically superb weapons produced by Germany during the 1930s and 1940s, the MG 34 and MG 42 could never prevent a final defeat of the Third Reich.

## POST-WAR IMPACT

War may have ceased in Europe in May 1945, but there was much life left in the MG 34 and MG 42. The quality of the design in the two weapons, and massive war-surplus stocks floating around in a tense, post-conflict world, meant that these great German machine guns would soon be gripped by many new hands. The MG 34 was the less successful of the two guns in terms of use after 1945. Being a more complicated, expensive and temperamental weapon than the MG 42, the MG 34 was not ideally suited to a long career in the Cold War context, but it still found fresh users. There is some evidence that numbers of Soviet- and British-captured MG 34s found their way into Chinese hands (both Kuomintang and People's Liberation Army) during both World War II and the Chinese Civil War (1927–50), and hence also appeared in limited numbers in the Korean War (1950–53). Other Chinese stocks might even have been purchased from countries such as Czechoslovakia, which continued to manufacture the MG 34 after the war as well as sell its wartime stocks. (The Germans produced the MG 34 in Czechoslovakia at Waffenwerke Brunn AG, Brno, from the late 1930s.) Interestingly, Czech-produced or reconditioned German MG 34s were also bought by Israel between 1947 and 1949, to boost the firepower of the country's nascent army as it achieved independence. The contracts included sales of 5,515 MG 34s, 10,000 ammunition belts and millions of rounds of 7.92×57mm ammunition.

Significant numbers of war-surplus MG 34s were sold to Israel in the late 1940s. Here we see one of these weapons, pintle-mounted on an Israeli Navy vessel in October 1948. (Cody Images)

MG 34s endured in small numbers in Israeli service through the 1950s and 1960s, serving in the Six-Day War of 1967. There are even some eyewitnesses who testify to MG 34s serving as position defence weapons into the 1980s. Note that the Czech suppliers weren't particularly fussy about who they sold MG 34s to – another post-war customer was Syria, which would quickly turn the barrels of its guns on similarly armed Israeli soldiers during various conflicts. Other Czech MG 34s were used by the *Front de Libération Nationale* (FLN; National Liberation Front) during its independence war against the French in Algeria in the 1950s and '60s. Evidently the Soviet bloc was not entirely concerned about the destination of its arms sales.

The Cold War connection meant that the MG 34 saw further combat use in South-East Asia, in the hands of the Viet Minh and then the Viet Cong in Indochina/Vietnam. Only some of these weapons flowed into Vietnamese communist hands from the Soviets or Chinese. Many were actually captured from the French, who relied substantially on requisitioned German small arms to equip its economically ravaged army following the end of the war in Europe. In fact, the MG 34 was found in some surprising corners of the globe, as many nations looked to obtain this first-rate infantry weapon. It was purchased by many African nations engaged in post-colonial struggles during the 1950s and '60s, and the machine gun was also seen in the hands of Fidel Castro's rebels in Cuba during the latter stages of the Cuban Revolution (1953–59).

The MG 34's post-war commercial distribution is nevertheless completely overshadowed by that achieved by the MG 42. In its 7.62mm NATO formats, as the MG3 or similar types, it has found new mounts, new purposes and, sadly, new conflicts in which to express its capabilities. Adopters or producers of the MG3 are truly diverse, and include Argentina, Australia, Bangladesh, Chile, Denmark, Estonia, Greece, Iran, Italy, Mexico, Myanmar, Norway, Pakistan, Spain, Sudan and Turkey. Many of these modern-day MG 42s have served in the traditional bipod-mounted LMG format, or on modified versions (sometimes scarcely so,

A Danish soldier is here seen in 1986 with an MG 42/59, designated the M/62 in the Danish Army. A spare barrel is lying across the barrel jacket. (Cody Images)

such was the quality of the original design) of the Lafette tripod. Yet MG3s have also been incorporated into all manner of new vehicles and platforms. In the Australian Army, the Leopard AS1 tank, adopted in 1976, was armed with no fewer than two MG3s, one fitted as a coaxial weapon, the other on the commander's hatch. Similarly, the Canadian, Finnish and Brazilian forces also used the MG3 in their own versions of the Leopard. MG3s have been mounted on a broad spectrum of other armoured vehicles, such as armoured personnel carriers (APCs) and infantry fighting vehicles (IFVs). The Norwegian armed forces, in addition to using the MG3 as a standard infantry weapon since 1969, have pintle-mounted versions on APCs and also in helicopters, much in the same way as the Finnish Army has applied MG3s to its NH-90 helicopters and Italy has fitted the MG 42/59 to various rotary-wing aircraft, such as the Agusta-Bell AB 212. The Italian Navy has MG 42/59s fitted to the guard rails of some of its ships. (One interesting point about the Italian armed forces is that they have recently brought out a version of the MG 42/59 modified to fire 5.56×45mm NATO ammunition, trading in the 7.62mm round's long-range firepower for an increase in the volume of ammunition that can be carried into battle.) We have also seen how the Bundeswehr adapted the MG3 to fit the latest generation of remote-control fire platforms, enabling machine-gunners to deliver heavy firepower from inside an armoured, protected environment via computerized fire control. German vehicles that rely on the MG3 include the Puma AIFV and the ATF Dingo infantry mobility vehicle.

What such adaptations, and numerous others, have achieved is in effect to keep the MG 42 fighting wars more than 70 years after it was first introduced. Illegal supplies have added to the MG 42's grim history of killing, often through circuitous routes. For example, Pakistan Ordnance Factories (POF) began a licensed production of the MG3 in the 1960s.

Danish soldiers of the International Security Assistance Force (ISAF) in Afghanistan patrol with an M/62 as their heavy firepower. Note that the optical sight of the MG3 can take a variety of day and night optics. (Cody Images)

Soldiers of a Bundeswehr mechanized infantry unit deploy their MG1A3, a form of the MG1 modified to take the 7.62×51mm NATO cartridge. The gunner's comrade is armed with a G3 rifle of the same calibre. (Cody Images)

The weapon subsequently went to war against India during the conflicts of the 1970s, and against terrorist groups in the northern tribal areas. Yet Pakistani MG3s also found their way, in limited numbers, into the hands of Mujahideen and Taliban fighters in Afghanistan, the insurgents potentially facing Bundeswehr troops armed with the same weapons. Insurgent groups in Iraq have also acquired numbers of MG3s. The most likely source of these weapons is Iran, which began licensed manufacture of the MG1A3 during the 1970s and continues the production and sale of the weapon to this day. Iran being classified by many Western nations as a sponsor of terrorism, many states are naturally not happy about the destinations of these guns.

The upshot of all this trade in MG 42 variants has been the gun's continued presence on the battlefield. The break-up of the former Yugoslavia in the 1990s saw thousands of licence-produced M53 machine

Post-war Panzergrenadier troops train with the 7.62mm MG3. When the Bundeswehr was formed, its ordnance authorities decided that the MG 42 could not be bettered by the existing crop of machine guns on the market. (Cody Images)

guns used on all sides of the conflict, including in some of the atrocities that blighted the country in those terrible years. The following account comes from testimony delivered at the International Criminal Tribunal for the former Yugoslavia, held in the late 1990s, as on 22 March 1999 the witness explains his encounter with a truck carrying Muslim soldiers in 1993:

> Q. Please tell us, in relation to the Prosecutor's questions that were put to you in connection with the truck that you saw, if you remember the one that you saw come into the village sometime in May 1992?
> A. Yes.
> Q. You said that you saw some boxes and a few rifles.
> A. Yes.
> Q. Tell me, did you see someone on the truck?
> A. Yes. Yes, I think I said so. I saw three Muslims, and they were there.
> Q. Did they have any weapons in their hands?
> A. I remember very well that one of them had a M53 machine gun in his hands and it surprised me.

The account goes on to explain how local state military arsenals had been overrun by both civilians and militias, turning large volumes of firearms and ammunition into various hands. The witness also explains hearing automatic fire around his locality, as the country collapsed into civil war.

MG 42s have similarly fuelled rebels, insurgents and wayward armies in many other parts of the world. In Myanmar, the indigenous MG3 produced by Ka Pa Sa has played a role in helping to suppress dissident factions among the population, and the Sudanese KARAR (an MG3 clone) has been used against factions in the war-torn region of Darfur. Born into the hands of one of the most disciplined and professional armies in history, the MG 42 has found its way into less controlled hands during the late 20th and early 21st centuries.

A US Marine inspects a German MG3 in Iraq. Note how the stock has been cut down; the gun could well have been mounted on an armoured vehicle. (Cody Images)

# CONCLUSION

German troops fire the MG3 from a Lafette tripod little different from ones that mounted MG 42s during World War II. A spare barrel lies on a container to the side; the container is designed to aid a hot barrel to cool quickly. (Cody Images)

Given the numbers of MG 34 and MG 42 weapons, and derivatives, produced from the mid-1930s to the present day, and the intrinsic integrity of the original design, these firearms are likely to remain with us for many years to come. Indeed, outside official use with armies, the guns keep cropping up in various odd contexts. Battlefield archaeologists, and eager amateurs armed with metal detectors, continue to unearth much-rusted specimens of these weapons from forgotten corners of World War II battlefields. Fully functioning wartime-era guns are also out there, still

74

hammering away on ranges and even in some military hands. For example, a story carried by the Associated Press on 22 March 2011 recounted that customs officials in Vilnius, Lithuania, had come across a complete and working MG 42 wrapped up in a package in Vilnius International Airport. The gun had been packaged up in Lithuania and was destined for an address in Germany, returning home, albeit illegally, after many years abroad.

The Internet continues to fuel enthusiasm for the MG 34 and MG 42, in terms of both sale and popularity. YouTube is replete with clips of shooters demonstrating both guns, particularly in the United States (at least in those states more amenable to the ownership of full-auto firearms). There is also a bubbling trade in MG 34 and MG 42 spare parts, and especially Yugoslavian M53 components, which enable enthusiasts to keep their weapons working after many years of service.

At the time of writing, the MG3 is in the early stages of being replaced in the Bundeswehr. The gas-operated 5.56mm MG4, looking very much like the Belgian Minimi, is the likeliest contender to become the standard squad support weapon and secondary armament on infantry fighting vehicles (it has been in Bundeswehr service since 2001). Unlike the MG3, it can be more comfortably operated by one man, and its reduced weight (8.1kg) and lighter ammunition make it more transportable around the battlefield, regardless of the physical stature of the operator. The HK 121, another weapon from the Heckler & Koch stable, is also jockeying for position, and provides a more interesting comparison with the MG3. It is a gas-operated weapon with a quick-detachable barrel and side-folding shoulder stock, but continues with the *Einheitsmaschinengewehr* concept. Its calibre is 7.62×51mm NATO, and it can take a variety of feed options,

The Heckler & Koch HK 121 is a possible replacement for the MG3 in Bundeswehr service. It still represents the principles of the *Einheitsmaschinengewehr*, being a true general-purpose machine gun. (KrisfromGermany)

from standard belts to 50-round containers. It can switch through the LMG, MMG and HMG roles according to the mount used, and it can even be mounted on MG3 tripods. The modern Picatinny accessories rail on the top of the gun allows fitment of different sight options, including thermal-imaging night-fighting instruments.

Only time and war will tell whether the Bundeswehr will evolve to have the correct firepower balance in its infantry squads. Combat experience in Afghanistan, however, suggests that the future weapons have a hard act to follow in the MG3. Lieutenant-Colonel Detlef Rausch, director of Infantry Future Development, German Infantry School, explained in 2010 how the MG3 delivered a genuine battlefield advantage in engagements with the Taliban:

> Lt. Col. Rausch said, 'In most cases the opponent fires first. The ammunition documentation on our side is quite high and the effectiveness of our weapons, especially at ranges exceeding 200m and against targets in defilade does not meet our expectations. The level of protection of both our vehicles and our equipment is however good. The Marder's armament has proved effective and other vehicles will soon be equipped with an automatic grenade launcher and heavy machine gun.'
>
> The opponent typically retains the initiative, making effective use of cover and blends with the indigenous population to avoid being engaged by mortar artillery or aircraft fire. The Taliban vary their methods between sniper fire at ranges of 800–1,500m, AK-47 in salvos at ranges exceeding 300m and opening fire at very close ranges between zero and 20m. Lt. Col. Rausch said that the current approach of the enemy is typically to engage friendly force with long range small arms weapons, even at ranges exceeding 300m which requires the capability at the infantry section level to engage selected targets at ranges at up to 600m. He commented, 'Reports from theatre say that the target effectiveness of 5.56mm standard rounds at ranges exceeding 300m is insufficient. Troops in theatre use the 7.62mm MG3 machine gun to engage enemy targets at ranges greater than 300m. Furthermore, some designated marksmen at squad level have been equipped with 7.62mm G3 rifles with telescopic sights for the engagement of individual targets. In the medium term, the German infantry needs follow on weapons to replace the MG3 and the G3 rifle.' (MacBarnet 2011: 9–11)

The need to reach out to targets at and beyond 300m is very clear from this account, and while the 5.56mm guns can deliver adequate punch up to 600m, beyond that their penetration and stability can drop dramatically. While the MG3 can appear quite dated in terms of its furniture and layout when compared to the new generations of squad automatic weapons, it still delivers a highly convincing combat performance across the range spectrum. Replacing it with a model that soldiers can trust equally will not be easy.

# GLOSSARY

**BLOWBACK**  A system of firearms operation that uses the breech pressure generated upon firing to operate the bolt

**BOLT**  The part of a firearm that closes the breech of the firearm and often performs the functions of loading, extraction and (via a firing pin) ignition

**BREECH**  The rear end of a gun barrel

**BREECH BLOCK**  A mechanism designed to close the breech for firing; roughly analogous to 'bolt'

**CARBINE**  A shortened rifle

**CHAMBER**  The section at the rear of the barrel into which the cartridge is seated for firing

**CLOSED BOLT**  Refers to firearms in which the bolt/breech block is closed up to the chamber before the trigger is pulled

**COOK-OFF**  The involuntary discharge of a cartridge by the build-up of heat in the chamber from firing

**DELAYED BLOWBACK**  A blowback mechanism in which the recoil of the bolt is mechanically delayed while the chamber pressures drop to safe levels

**EJECTOR**  The mechanism that throws an empty cartridge case clear of a gun following extraction from the chamber

**EXTRACTOR**  The mechanism that removes an empty cartridge case from the chamber after firing

**GAS OPERATION**  A system of operating the cycle of a firearm using gas tapped off from burning propellant

**LOCK TIME**  The time interval between pulling the trigger and the gun firing

**OPEN BOLT**  Refers to firearms in which the bolt/breech block is held back from the breech before the trigger is pulled

**RECEIVER**  The main outer body of a gun, which holds the firearm's action

**RECOIL OPERATED**  An automatic weapon powered through the extraction, ejection and loading cycles by the forces of recoil. In a short-recoil weapon, the barrel and bolt recoil for less than the length of a cartridge before they unlock and ejection takes place

**SEMI-AUTOMATIC**  A weapon that fires one round and reloads ready for firing with every pull of the trigger

# BIBLIOGRAPHY & FURTHER READING

**Primary sources, printed and electronic:**

Oberkommando des Heeres (1944), *Training Manual for the MG 42 as a Light and Heavy Machine Gun (Weapon Training)*, September 1944.

US Army (1943). Military Intelligence Service. Special Series No. 14, 25 May 1943.

US Army (1944a). *Tactical and Technical Trends*, No. 42, 13 January 1944 (<http://www.lonesentry.com/articles/ttt09/mg42-firing-data.html>, accessed 15 March 2012).

US Army (1944b). Military Intelligence Service. 'A German Defense on the Anzio Front', *Intelligence Bulletin*, July 1944 (<http://www.lonesentry.com/articles/gedefarea/index.html>, accessed 15 March 2012).

US Army (1944c). 329th Infantry Regiment, 'Action Against Enemy, Reports After' (After Action Report), 8 August 1944.

US War Department (1943). TM E9-206A, *German 7.9-mm Dual Purpose Machine Gun MG 34*, 13 April 1943.

**Primary sources, audiovisual:**

International Criminal Tribunal for the Former Yugoslavia, 22 March 1999.

US War Department Film Bulletin F.B. No. 181, *Automatic Weapons: American vs. German*, 1944.

**Secondary sources:**

Bull, Stephen (2005). *World War II Infantry Tactics: Company and Battalion*. Oxford: Osprey Publishing.

Burney, Sgt Jazz (2011). 'Vanguard Soldiers earn *Schutzenschnur* [sic]'. *The Bayonet*, Vol. 1, Issue 4 (June 2011), 5–6.

Erenberger, Timothy (2000). *Grandfather's Tale: The Tale of a German Sniper*. Bloomington, IN: iUniverse.

Flower, Desmond & James Reeves, eds (1960). *The War 1939–1945: A Documentary History*. London: Cassell.

Ford, Roger (1999). *The World's Great Machine Guns: From 1860 to the Present Day*. London: Brown Books.

Freidlin, Seymour & William Richardson, eds (1958). *The Fatal Decisions*. New York, NY: Berkley.

Happe, Heinrich (1957). *Moscow Tram Stop*. London: Collins.

Hartman, Bernd (2010). *Panzers in the Sand: The History of Panzer Regiment 5, 1935–1941*, Volume 1. Mechanicsburg, PA: Stackpole.

Hogg, Ian & John Weeks (1991). *Military Small Arms of the 20th Century*. London: Arms & Armour Press.

MacBarnet, Don (2011). 'The Ballistics of ISAF Weapons during Operation Enduring Freedom'. *Ballistic Testing and Instrumentation*. London: Global Business Media, 9–11.

Mazgai, Marian S. (2008). *In the Polish Secret War: Memoir of a World War II Freedom Fighter*. Jefferson, NC: McFarland.

Myrvang, Folke (2002). *MG 34 – MG 42: German Universal Machine Guns*, ed. R. Blake Stevens. Cobourg: Collector Grade Publications.

Renouf, Tom (2011). *Black Watch: Liberating Europe and Catching Himmler – My Extraordinary WW2 with the Highland Division*. London: Hachette.

Sajer, Guy (1977). *The Forgotten Soldier*. London: Sphere Books.

Schulman, Milton (1947). *Defeat in the West*. London: Secker & Warburg.

Scislowski, Stanley (1997). *Not All of Us Were Brave*. Toronto: Dundurn Press.

Shaw, Irwin (1946). *St. Lô*. American Forces in Action Series. Washington, DC: US Army Center of Military History.

Taylor, Thomas & Robert J. Martin (1997). *Rangers: Lead the Way*. Nashville, TN: Turner Publishing Co.

Walter, John (2004). *Guns of the Third Reich*. London: Greenhill.

# INDEX